FROM
# COMPLICITY
TO
# ENCOUNTER

# Christian Mission and Modern Culture

EDITED BY
ALAN NEELY, H. WAYNE PIPKIN,
AND WILBERT R. SHENK

In the Series:

*Living Faithfully in a Fragmented World,*
by Jonathan R. Wilson

*Into the Vacuum,*
by Gordon Scoville

*Speaking the Truth in Love,*
by James V. Brownson

*From Complicity to Encounter,*
by Jane Collier and Rafael Esteban

*Canon and Mission,*
by H. D. Beeby

*The Missiological Implications of
Epistemological Shifts,*
by Paul G. Hiebert

First published by
TRINITY PRESS INTERNATIONAL
P.O. Box 1321
Harrisburg, PA 17105
U.S.A.

Trinity Press International is a division of The Morehouse Group.

Scripture quotations are from The New Jerusalem Bible, (General Editor, Henry Wansbrough), London; Darton, Lougman and Todd 1985.

Cover design: Brian Preuss

**Library of Congress Cataloging-in-Publication Data**

Collier, Jane, 1936–
    From complicity to encounter : the church and the
    culture of economism / Jane Collier, Rafael Esteban.
        p.   cm. -- (Christian mission and modern culture)
    Includes bibliographical references.
    ISBN 1-56338-260-1
    1. Missions—Theory. 2. Catholic Church—Missions.
3. Christianity and culture.   4. Economics—Religious
aspects—Catholic Church. I. Esteban, Rafael, 1939–   .
II. Title. III. Series.
BV2180.C588  1998
261.8'5—dc21                    98-48833
                                   CIP

*Printed in the United States of America*
98  99  00  01  02  6  5  4  3  2  1

# FROM
# *COMPLICITY*
# TO
# *ENCOUNTER*

## The Church and the Culture of Economism

———

## JANE COLLIER
## RAFAEL ESTEBAN

TRINITY PRESS
INTERNATIONAL
HARRISBURG, PENNSYLVANIA

Write the vision down;
Inscribe it on tablets
To be easily read.
Since this vision
Is for its own time only
Eager for its own fulfillment.
It does not deceive!
If it comes slowly, wait,
For come it will,
Without fail.

Habakkuk 2:2–3

# Contents

6.78

96374

# Preface to the Series

Both Christian mission and modern culture, widely regarded as antagonists, are in crisis. The emergence of the modern mission movement in the early nineteenth century cannot be understood apart from the rise of technocratic society. Now, at the end of the twentieth century, both modern culture and Christian mission face an uncertain future.

One of the developments integral to modernity was the way the role of religion in culture was redefined. Whereas religion had played an authoritative role in the culture of Christendom, modern culture was highly critical of religion and increasingly secular in its assumptions. A sustained effort was made to banish religion to the backwaters of modern culture.

The decade of the 1980s witnessed further momentous developments on the geopolitical front with the collapse of communism. In the aftermath of the breakup of the system of power blocs that dominated international relations for a generation, it is clear that religion has survived even if its institutionalization has undergone deep change and its future forms are unclear. Secularism continues to oppose religion, while technology has emerged as a major source of power and authority in modern culture. Both confront Christian faith with fundamental questions.

The purpose of this series is to probe these developments from a variety of angles with a view to helping the church understand its missional responsibility to a culture in crisis. One important resource is the church's experience of two centuries of cross-cultural mission that has reshaped the church into a global Christian *ecumene*. The focus of our inquiry will be the church in modern culture. The series (1) examines modern/postmodern culture from a missional point of view; (2) develops the theological agenda that the church in modern culture must address in order to recover its own integrity; and (3) tests fresh conceptualizations of the nature and mission of the church as it engages modern culture. In other words, these volumes are intended to be a forum where conventional assumptions can be challenged and alternative formulations explored.

This series is a project authorized by the Institute of Mennonite Studies, research agency of the Associated Mennonite Biblical Seminary, and supported by a generous grant from the Pew Charitable Trusts.

*Editorial Committee*

ALAN NEELY
H. WAYNE PIPKIN
WILBERT R. SHENK

# Introduction

On a recent phone-in on a Roman Catholic religious-affairs radio program from somewhere in the United States, a caller asked why it was that a church that had sent thousands of missionaries all over the world seemed unable to preach the gospel effectively in the United States. The presenter was clearly not ready for the question, and she fudged the answer. Weren't six billion people "out there" somehow more important as mission targets than a mere three hundred million, she argued, for doesn't scripture lay on us the duty of preaching to the whole world? Admittedly, the radio talk show wasn't the kind of program where difficult questions and controversial issues find a sympathetic platform, but we had hoped for at least some kind of substantive answer simply because the question was also our question, the question that has prompted not only the writing of this book but also the creation of the series in which it appears.

Missiologists tell us that this question has no easy answer (Bosch 1991), but it nevertheless has to be taken seriously. Answers need explanations, and explanation requires understanding. Understanding of anything so complex has to be based on mental maps, analogies, models (Hesse 1980). Although in themselves these give an irrevocable shape to the subject they encourage the beginnings of an understanding on which it is possible to base explanations. Our attempts at understanding always start from a determinate standpoint. In our case what we have to say is based on our own particular Christian experience as Roman Catholics; others will start their reflection from the experience of different Christian traditions, but they will make similar journeys in their search for understanding. But this does not imply that we arrive at different endpoints. As Christians we share the question, the problem; the understanding we seek must be holistic rather than particular.

We begin to map out the terrain of the question by choosing the notion of "culture" as the root metaphor by which we conceptualize the "world" that is addressed by the gospel. Our approach to culture is deliberately artistic as opposed to analytic because one can thereby create more meaning with fewer words (Bateson 1958).

> The artist is content to describe culture in such a manner that many of its premises and the inter-relations of its parts are implicit in his composition. He can leave a great many of the most fundamental aspects of culture to be picked up, not from his actual words, but from his emphasis. He can choose words whose sound is more significant than their dictionary meaning, and he can so group and stress them that the reader almost unconsciously receives information which is not explicit in the sentences and which the artist would find it hard—almost impossible—to express in analytic terms (Bateson 1958:1).

The analytic license permitted by this approach allows us to characterize Western culture as a "culture of economism." In order to explore what this means in practice, we have to get a sense of the way in which the culture works, and so we create another "mental map" that allows us to describe the functioning of cultures in terms of managing their value dilemmas in such a way that the culture strengthens and flourishes.

The concept of culture can be applied at a variety of levels, from the global to the group. Mission is the task of the institutional church, which insofar as it has organizational characteristics can itself be described as a culture; it therefore also faces the task of managing its own internal value dilemmas. We argue that the failure of mission to Western culture is due to the symbiosis between the ambiguities that lie deep in the culture of economism and those that are manifest in the organizational culture of the church (particularly the Roman Catholic Church). Both are power cultures that share a history of conquest and oppression; both have disregarded the cultural imperative to use their value diversities and dilemmas as ways of creating cultural harmony and creative synergy.

But there have been signs of hope in both camps—cultural paradigm shifts at the organizational level in both church and economism. It is in these paradigm shifts that we see a window of opportunity for mission, but mission understood not in terms of the traditional understandings of missionary activity but in terms of the metaphor of encounter. We see this understanding of mission not only as reflecting the reality of missionary experience but also as paradigmatic of the whole gospel narrative.

It is not without significance that we have chosen to collaborate on this book. We come from different disciplines and different cultural traditions, but we believe that synergy comes from the encounter of differences. One of us has a granddaughter, Nancy, who when she was three habitually referred to God as "him-and-her" because, as she pointed out, "we have she's and he's in my kindergarten." She may be no theologian of the Trinity, but she has spotted a profound truth. It is in the spirit of the search for that truth that we undertake this collaboration.

# 1

# The Crisis of Western Culture and Christian Mission

As we approach the new millennium, we are aware of the fact that our world is experiencing a crisis whose scale and urgency are without parallel in recorded history.[1] Every aspect of our lives is threatened by irreversible and uncontrollable forces—environmental deterioration, political and economic instability, social disintegration, human repression, nuclear proliferation, and the uncontrolled expansion of the arms trade. Familiar ways of living are being replaced by more uncertain modes of existence; and for increasing numbers of people, even in the so-called rich countries, there is little hope of a settled existence. In the church in particular, there are many who view the present crisis with trepidation. They see a church in danger of being engulfed under waves of secularism and materialism, with a loss of so-called traditional values and a weakening of ecclesial authority and influence. Their response is to retreat to the old certainties. But such "restorationism" does not constitute an adequate Christian response to the crisis of our world. A more positive attitude is needed, because that very crisis, and in particular the crisis of Western culture itself, constitutes the greatest challenge yet encountered by Christian mission.

4

Are we confident that as Christians we can meet that challenge? After all, there are many ways in which Christian mission is itself in crisis (Bosch 1991). We should perhaps take consolation from the knowledge that the Chinese word for crisis—wei-ji—is made up of the characters for "danger" and "opportunity," and that from a historical perspective crisis has often been the messenger of transformation. Christian mission may be facing a challenge, but it may also be facing its greatest opportunity yet, an opportunity to witness to the saving power of Christ in a world that more than ever before needs to be saved from itself. In order to take up this challenge, two things are needed. First, the Christian church must develop a profound understanding of the cultural context of its mission to Western culture and of its own role within that culture. Second, it has to discern what mission in that cultural context might entail. This book aims to contribute to the development of these understandings.

Mission is the encounter of two evolving and transforming realities. It takes place when a human frontier is crossed, when the missionary builds the Kingdom in another culture, another language (Shorter 1988). It is through mission that the church reaches out and meets human beings who are already shaped by their own cultures, but it addresses culture as the location of shared meanings. It is our culture that gives us the symbolic and linguistic richness we need to hear the word of God, to see with the eyes of our mind. Scripture recognizes this; it couches the metaphorical understanding of the way in which we receive the Good News in terms of "seeing" and "hearing." Jesus opened the eyes of the blind and the ears of the deaf; Paul speaks of the way in which God enlightens the eyes of our mind (Eph 1:18). But our seeing and hearing are not simple and physical; what we see and hear is the complexity of God's Word in Jesus as shaped by our cultural perceptions. The gospel we preach to others is culturally embedded, and those who hear it need their own interpretative grids—a symbolic system, a language—in order to hear it.

Mission thus requires an understanding of culture that is eclectic in the sense that it draws on interpretations that are proper to different disciplines, but which is also capable of articulation and practical application. There is no shortage of relevant images. Culture is a way of being human, a "design for living" (Kluckhorn 1969), learned and transmitted within groups as beliefs, values and customs. It is the order, or framework, that is both cause and result of a plurality of interpretative interactions (Alexander and Seidman 1990:1). It is the "webs of significance" within and by which people seek meaning and purpose in their lives (Geertz 1973). Or, to use a more evocative and contemporary analogy, it is the "software of the mind" (Hofstede 1991).

One way of visualizing this complexity is to think of the various aspects of culture as layered, rather like an onion. At the core, the deepest layer of culture, are the presuppositions, the cultural worldview that shapes perceptions, as well as the values that dictate notions of what is good. More superficial layers represent the different ways in which culture is enacted—the language and symbols that carry cultural meaning, the rituals by which it is expressed, the norms of behavior and social interaction. The outer visible layers consist of cultural "products"—art, architecture, commodities, as well as the institutions that support cultural coherence.[2] Institutions are important as cultural transmitters because they ensure that people construe experience in the same way; they serve to select, structure, and transmit culturally valued meanings and thus perpetuate a stable and meaningful order.

If we reflect on our own Western culture, we realize that culture not only is layered, but also manifests itself at different levels—the national, the regional, the generational, the social, the organizational. Each one of us embodies a mix of these cultural influences, and the different concerns that they reflect contribute to the richness of our cultural diversity. However, in the context of Western culture as a whole there are three cultural "fingerprints" that are relevant to the understanding of the complexity of mission. The first of these is that the culture is elitist. The consensus of values and beliefs has been regarded as something so important that its preservation and dissemination is safeguarded by "elites" who refine and define what constitutes "high culture." High culture is for the few; the assumption is that the rest are "uncultured." This classicist conception of culture contrasts with empiricist notions that see culture as a set of meanings and values that inform a way of life,[3] but it underlies the thinking of writers such as T. S. Eliot (1948), who perceived culture (high) to be in decline at the same time as he argued that every social class has its own culture. Half a century later we no longer subscribe to Eliot's idyllic vision of popular culture; what we see is mass culture, where the individual is powerless against the economic and technological forces of late Western capitalism,[4] where meanings and values are created by the media, and where autonomy and creativity are suppressed by the "culture industry," whose primary purpose is to maintain consumption levels.

The second characteristic of Western culture is that it is divisive. The dynamics of cultural transmission create social relations of inequality and power because some are more able to decipher cultural codes than are others. Families and educational institutions transmit these cultural codes, but they have unequal access to the richness and depth of the culture because they are differently privileged. The ability of children to assimilate cultural conditioning varies not just because of ability but also because of accidents of birth and upbringing. Institutional transmission thus serves to perpetuate the socially conditioned inequalities of cultural competence that determine the inequalities of success in any society (Bourdieu 1990). Western culture values success above all else: there is no place for the human diversity represented by weakness.

The third fingerprint is the imperialism of Western culture. The culture we all share—European culture alias Western culture alias modernity—has shaped most of the world through complex alliances of economic, religious, and political interests. In the process it has all but abolished cultural diversity across nation-states, and threatens to abolish it at the global level. In parts of the world where Western culture is a recent phenomenon—for instance, in Africa—the process of cultural disintegration is particularly marked. For young people, and for those who want to "get on," becoming a person of culture has come to mean buying into the aesthetic, literary, and philosophical premises of Western culture. Education has meant abandoning the vernacular language, learning cultural myths that have little relevance to the realities of everyday existence, and eventually distancing oneself from, even rejecting, cultural roots. The resultant weakening of cultural diversity has been reinforced by the homogenization created by universal education, urbanization, and the spread of mass communication, as well as by the fragmentation that is the consequence of the demise of culture-as-community.

## A Theology of Culture

In order to understand the dynamic of the missionary encounter, we need more than an understanding of culture; we also need a theology of culture. Theological reflection on culture begins from the fundamental premise that all cultures are ambiguous; they are at the same time "symbolic" and "diabolic."[5] On the one hand, cultures institutionalize, under the guidance of the spirit that inhabits every heart, everything that helps to grow, to personalize, and to build the community that enables human flourishing. In this sense they are symbolic; they bring together, they unite, they heal, they are life giving and life sustaining. On the other hand, like every human reality, cultures are under the inexorable law of death, in that they are continually threatened by the decay and disintegration of what is good. In one word, they are diabolic. The diabolic side of cultures is manifested only too clearly in their potential for death and destruction, for exclusivity and intolerance, for institutionalizing oppression and injustice, for justifying the raw use of power, for exploiting the poor, for debasing women, for wasting the earth, for penalizing dissent, for idolizing the individual, for banning dreams and dreamers, for stoning and crucifying prophets.

Even "Christian cultures" are ambiguous. Every vision of the world and every faith, including Christianity, must express themselves in symbolic systems and thus become "cultures." Christian churches themselves live through a continuous process in which faith as the reception of the gospel searches for cultural expression. Christian cultures become, and continue to be, symbolic (life enhancing) in the measure that they are faithful to the gospel, even though they live with, and may never succeed in totally neutralizing, the diabolic. The history of Christianity demonstrates all too clearly that no culture is unambiguous and that Christian cultures can be as destructive and death dealing as others, even as they evoke the name of Jesus Christ in support of their actions.

All cultures are already "evangelized" in the measure that they are open to the symbolic action of God's spirit, which reconciles and draws all humankind together. At the same time, every culture needs an evangelization that challenges its diabolic tendencies. Such an evangelization is possible as long as there is cultural coherence, but from a theological point of view the real problem arises when cultures threaten to disintegrate, in the sense that they lose their symbolic side, their capacity for togetherness and community. This is what is happening in the rich countries of the world where community is being destroyed, where technology replaces values, where a flood of so-called information exiles wisdom, where "society" is considered irrelevant and is systematically destroyed to give free rein to the individual, where lost social cohesion is replaced progressively by police coercion, where a small minority claims total right to exploit the world, its peoples, and its resources at the cost of suffering and death on an apocalyptic scale, and where individual is pitted against individual in a frenetic pursuit of the accumulation of wealth and power. All of this goes under the name of "global culture," but it is better described as "anticulture," where the diabolic threatens to kill the symbolic. It is only because we believe in the power of God to recover the good in all human situations that we can speak of the possibility of Christian mission in such a cultural context.

## The Culture of Economism

Culture is both complex and simple. In order to discuss the problem of mission in the context of the ambiguity of Western culture we need (1) to develop an initial "feel" for the culture,[6] (2) to be able to identify some kind of cultural "ethos" (Bateson 1984),[7] and (3) to characterize the culture's "configuration" (Benedict 1935). The overriding perspective in the apparent complexity is the cultural importance of the "economic."[8] It is the economic aspect of our lives that more than any other shapes our understanding, our evaluations, and our aspirations, and hence conditions our actions. It is the economic that generates our culture's rituals and defines our symbols. Our language conveys the depth of that influence; our cultural stories— our myths—are stories about wealth, success and power, progress, growth and prosperity. Our institutions, whether they be business corporations or hospitals or universities or charity foundations, are run on economic criteria. Even our personal lives are shaped by calculations of value, of gain and cost, of sound investment and satisfaction of wants. Economic issues prevail in the media; rewards for work are measured in monetary terms, virtue is defined in terms of economic success; consumerism rules the pursuit of leisure. Western culture can thus be characterized as a "culture of economism." Economism, says the Oxford English Dictionary, "imposes the primacy of economic causes or factors as the main source of cultural meanings and values." Pope John Paul II uses the term *economism* frequently to designate the nexus of materialistic values.[9] But economism is more than a set of values; it is the whole cultural package.

At the core of this cultural "onion" are the presuppositions, often unconsciously held, that lie at the root of all our thinking.[10] These presuppositions represent our worldview, our "cosmology," and they are grounded in the cultural belief in science. The discipline of economics, which has gradually been developed over the past two centuries as a way of explaining economic existence, relies heavily on this worldview, and the cultural thought-forms of economism are drawn from and articulated by that discipline. The scientific worldview is based on the belief that there is an external world made up of objects; a world ordered according to laws of nature reflected in causal processes. We believe that it is possible to access this world, to understand and know it in terms of categories and concepts, and to restate its features as knowledge claims or facts in the form of true and unconditional propositions. We have a profound faith in the power of science to establish what is unambiguously and objectively "the case"; in other words, we believe that truth can be not only sought but also actually attained. We are therefore justified in believing that science can change the world and that progress is possible. This is our core cultural myth; it enables us to trust in our own power to control our destiny;

it represents our insurance and our psychological security in the face of mounting evidence of our own powerlessness.

Our conviction that science is true because it is powerful easily becomes a conviction that science represents the only cognitive access to reality, so that only what is seen can be believed, only what is proved can be true. We have lost the ability to recognize the reality and truth conveyed by myth or symbol: scientific beliefs fulfill the functions that mythic accounts, including biblical myths, fulfilled in earlier societies. In fact, an important myth in our culture is that mythology itself is worthless because it is nonrational. Not only does this worldview challenge the possibility of faith in God, but it impoverishes our self-understanding because it limits our idea of our own personhood to what is scientifically accessible (Collier 1990, 1992).

Economics has always attempted to ally itself with the scientific enterprise in order to demonstrate its epistemological legitimacy, and its models of the world are based on the presuppositions of the scientific worldview.[11] "Economics prides itself on its science-like character, and economists on their ability to speak like scientists, without color, passion or values" (Heilbronner 1988:38). Neoclassical economics, which remains unchallenged as the ruling paradigm,[12] resembles Newtonian physics in structural and conceptual terms. The structural "iconic" metaphor is that of the giant machine we call the market. Adam Smith, the father of modern economics, saw the economy as a market mechanism where self-interested decisions of buyers and sellers would collectively create order and harmony: the intervention of the "invisible hand" would bring the mechanism to an equilibrium where the right goods were being sold at the right prices, so that public welfare and private gain would both be maximized.[13] Smith's ideas lent themselves to mathematical and therefore scientific law-like formulation by later economists, and thus enabled the use of calculus to give a precise formulation of the individual behavior patterns that supposedly underlay the workings of the market mechanism. Alfred Marshall, and the other giants of neoclassical economics expanded and enriched his views, and economists since then have adhered to these views in order to give "scientific" status to the discipline.

The "scientific" status of economics has always ensured its cultural and ideological standing. But economics clearly cannot be scientific in the generally accepted sense of the word.[14] It does not deal with the unchanging realities of the natural sciences; rather, it deals with people's unpredictable motivation and behavior in social and political contexts. People are unpredictable, moreover, what happens to them matters. The clash between the demands of scientific value-freedom and the reality of value-laden politics has always been resolved by maintaining the fact-value distinction, expressed in textbooks as the distinction between "positive" and "normative" economics, between "what is" and "what ought to be" in economic terms. Generations of economics students have been reared on this distinction, the root premise of positivism. It implies, first, that we can "do" scientific economics without taking any normative issues into account. It also implies that the epistemological status of positive and normative economics is different. Positive economics cannot be challenged because it is "hard," scientific, true—a matter of "fact." Normative economics, on the other hand, is "soft," nonscientific, and therefore to be taken lightly—a matter of "opinion." It is the positive-normative distinction that has served to exclude the realm of values from economics as a class of explanations.

### Economism as Ideology

The image of the market as the self-regulating mechanism that allocates scarce resources to their optimal use remains as metaphor and as ruling paradigm in the discipline today. It is also the basis of the ideological status of economics

(Heilbronner 1988, 1990).[15] The ideology of the last two decades has given us a mental map that depicts the economy, whether on a global or a national level, as a series of interlinked markets. Health care, child care, education— all are seen in terms of markets. This ideology gives a naturalistic shape to the complexity of social process. If markets are the natural form of economic interaction, then rationally—so the argument runs—they must be the right form. Anything that interferes with the free working of markets must therefore be wrong, and market processes should be introduced into situations where nonmarket economic interaction exists.

The ability of this ideology to maintain the hegemony of the market as an all-pervasive "theory of everything" rests on the prevalence in economics of the fact-value distinction, which allows social and political realities to be ignored. But even in terms of economic theory, the ideology has no basis. In the first place, the market in economic theory is a static concept that relies for its functioning on assumptions of no time (so that adjustment is instantaneous), no space (so that information to all market participants is perfect), and some kind of adjustment facility, such as an auction, so that the market-clearing trading price can be established. None of these assumptions hold true in practice. In other words, markets do not work in textbook fashion, they do not allocate optimally, and they often do not even exist because some goods cannot be allocated by the market.[16] Furthermore, existing markets are not "free" in a mechanistic sense, because they are frequently manipulated by the more powerful participants in order to gain at the expense of the weaker players. The best example of this is the operation of commodity markets, where suppliers frequently lose out because of the actions of powerful buyers.

Market ideology is rooted in individualism as the functional principle of the mechanistic economic universe.[17]

Individual action is seen as based on two guiding princi-
ples—self-interest and rationality. Rationality in this context simply means that people are assumed to do whatever
serves their own interests or "maximizes their utility." In
philosophical terms, this represents an extraordinarily narrow view of human rationality. It is also empty of any real
content because people are ruled by the determinisms of
the price mechanism, which allocates not only goods but
also life and work choices. It is this cultural belief that
rationality is an essential prerequisite for adequate human
functioning, combined with an eccentric understanding of
rationality as pursuing one's own self-interest, that has created the impoverished and reductionistic view of the
human person associated with the culture of economism.

The significance of all this is simply stated. The
thought-forms of "scientism" and of neoclassical economics shape our cultural worldview, as they were themselves
shaped by the worldviews of their time. They give us dominant images of reality that crowd out all alternative
images. We are culturally conditioned to believe in our ability to know, to manipulate and control, to solve our own
problems, to believe that facts are more important than
values, that the material matters more than the spiritual,
that material success is the measure of the "good life," and
that competition and acquisition are the ways to achieve it.
We also have a profound faith in the ability of technological change to create progress, growth, and prosperity by
providing new possibilities for economic expansion.

### The Language of Economism

How are these cultural thought-forms codified and transmitted? At one level, this is the job of culture's institutions—
families, educational establishments, ritualized gatherings
of all kinds. But at a deeper level it is language that shapes
and conditions cultural thinking. In our verbal culture, where
technological change has revolutionized communication

and information transmission, the explanation for the way in which the thought-forms of economism become cultur- ally pervasive is to be found above all in the extent to which the economic shapes our language. Language shapes and is shaped by culture: it gives form and content to our beliefs and feelings; it structures thought and hence action. The simplest example of this is the anthropological evi- dence that cultural concepts of time, space, and matter vary with the possibilities and limitations of the linguistic forms in which they are expressed.[18] Benjamin Whorf, who gathered much of this evidence, offers this reflection:

> Actually, thinking is most mysterious, and by far the greatest light we have is thrown by the study of lan- guage. This study shows that the forms of a person's thoughts are controlled by inexorable laws of pattern of which he is unconscious. These patterns are the unperceived systematizations of his own language— shown readily enough by a candid comparison and contrast with other languages, especially those of a different linguistic family.... And every language is a vast pattern system, different from others, in which are culturally ordained the forms and categories by which the personality not only communicates, but also analyses nature, notices or neglects types of relationship and phenomena, channels his reason- ing, and builds the house of his consciousness" (Whorf 1956:252).

Language is the grid that links reality with thought, the medium by which meaning is created and interpreted. Language is to culture what DNA is to reproduction; both carry the codes of evolution. We can live only as language allows us to think.

In Western culture it is to a large extent the economic that provides the ordinary-language terms and expressions that we use to give meaning to our world of daily life as we confront it, act in it, and live through it (Benton 1990:67). This happens on two levels. At one level, "economics talk" operates in several different ways to structure thought and hence action. In the first place, language affects economic reality insofar as we affect and change that reality by action that is based on understandings grounded in linguistic meaning (Samuels 1990).[19] Second, it is only through the language of economics that we can interpret that reality: economics thus functions as a hermeneutic by which we read reality, rather than as the objective science it understands itself to be (Heilbronner 1990). Third, it is by analyzing economics as discourse that we come to uncover the underlying preconceptions and structural understandings in economic theory, the "deep structure" of economic thought embedded noncognitively in the language of economists. And fourth, we have become increasingly aware of the way in which rhetoric is used to structure the nature and direction of disciplinary questioning, and by implication to restrict or eliminate certain areas of inquiry (Klamer et al., 1988).

At another and more profound level, our entire perception of reality is shaped by concept and metaphor, and our whole cultural understanding of the economic dimension of our lives is based on the ways in which we talk about it. Economic reality is in any case pretty elusive. The concepts we use to talk about the economic have no empirical content; economics suffers from a "crisis of abstraction"(Hutchinson 1977) in that reality can be accessed only as data. Data collection and presentation involve "category choice" in a way that inevitably implies the exclusion of other possibilities; data has to be simplified and homogenized in order to fit into chosen categories, and it is subject to problems of misrepresentation and nonreporting. Above all, data can be, and is, politically manipulated: the reality of unemployment and inflation depends on which figures are quoted. And if figures do not exist, the reality is inaccessible. Poverty no longer exists as an economic reality in the United Kingdom, because since 1988 poverty statistics are no longer collected; therefore, there is no empirical basis for discussion of poverty as a policy problem, even though poverty is visible on the streets of every city in the country.

There are also problems connected with establishing concept boundaries. When does a car stop being a car and become some other kind of vehicle? If unemployed means being without work for fourteen days, is the person who is without work for thirteen days employed during that period? This problem of "loose concepts" is best exemplified by the money supply. Definitions of the money supply proliferate and change with the exigencies of political expediency, with institutional change, and with theoretical fashion. However, economists convince us that they know what money is, and the whole world knows that inflation must be fought by reducing the money supply—usually by reducing public expenditure on health, education, and welfare. The human suffering this entails is effectively hidden behind the rhetoric of policy discussions on this issue.

### Economism as Metaphor

The real power of economic language to influence cultural perceptions and understandings derives from its status as metaphor. Metaphor creates culture-specific meanings and hence governs what we do and how we relate to others.[20] The essence of metaphor is the understanding and experiencing of one thing in terms of another, of the complex and obscure in terms of the experientially transparent. A good example of this is the metaphor "time is money," by which we are encouraged to think of time as valuable, because money is, but also as a limited resource that can be spent, saved, wasted. This concept of time has arguably contributed more to the Westernization of cultures than any other ordinary-language metaphor (Lakoff and Johnson

1980:137). Another example of the power of ordinary-language metaphor is the way in which we use direction to indicate value bias.[21] We tend to equate "more" with up, "good" with up, and thereby to perceive more as better. Until recently there has been an unquestioning acceptance in economics of the "goodness" of growth in income and output. This is an understanding that is underpinned by theory and conditions the attitudes of developed countries to Third World economies, in spite of all the evidence of the inappropriateness and destructiveness of "development."

What is important for the argument here is the kind of economic metaphors we use in everyday speech. The root metaphors by which we understand the workings of the economy are those given by theory. Metaphorical concepts such as equilibrium, elasticity, and market forces are generated by the mechanistic nature of microeconomic theory.[22] Macroeconomics relies much more on images derived from engineering: we talk about leakages from the circular flow of income, the velocity of circulation of money, the engine of growth, the balance of trade, an overheated economy, depression (Henderson 1982). It is these metaphors that give us an understanding of the economy as a working machine, a rotating engine, functioning independent of human volition.

Metaphor hides as well as elucidates aspects of experience, and one of the things economic metaphors frequently hide is the significance of the human.[23] The economy is conceived in terms not of people and what they do but of aggregates—consumer demand, unemployment. Labor is seen as a "resource," a "substance" to be quantified and "used up," a "factor of production" on a par with capital and land, to be discussed in terms of supply and price. Cheaper resources are desirable; therefore cheap labor is a good thing, and an "inexhaustible supply of cheap labor" in poorer countries can be discussed without ever considering the reality of the human degradation experienced by the people called "units of labor" by economics.

The opposite effect is seen in the way the nonhuman is personalized. Policy is "aggressive," profits "forge ahead," bond markets "look happier." Economies—and companies—are leaner and fitter when appropriate "diagnoses" of their problems are made and remedies are applied. Economies "suffer" when "wrong prescriptions" are applied to cure the "disease" of inflation, and structural adjustment is always "painful" but necessary, because inflation is the "enemy" we fear. These metaphors not only displace concern from the human to the nonhuman; they are also loaded with hidden bias. The disease metaphor, for instance, has been influential in persuading policy makers that urban areas suffer from "urban blight," which can be dealt with only by demolishing what is often architecturally worthwhile and initiating a process of "urban renewal." (The loss of much of Dublin's Georgian architectural heritage in the name of "progress" is still a matter of regret.)

Economic metaphor creeps into everyday understandings through its use as rhetoric (McCloskey 1994). Politicians know that the coherence of economic metaphor lends persuasive force to their arguments. Journalists use dramatic conventions—evil, suspense, heroics. Markets are excited or depressed; businessmen are courageous or creative; foreign countries are beating us in the race, defeating us in the battle, the United States is losing the contest in world markets. Genetic metaphors dominate the discussion of economic relationships. Competition is conflict and struggle for survival, markets are jungles, foreign competitors are predators, rivals must be resisted. The Darwinian bias creeps in where global "natural selection" via the international division of labor is seen as the inevitable outcome of the process. Company reports, too, are couched in terms of the language of the battlefield: strategic goals are set, orders are fought for, challenges are met, and battles are won. In this way we are encouraged to believe that stress and conflict are natural, realistic, and

unavoidable (Benton 1990). We come to understand ourselves as competitors driven by motives of wanting, having,
choosing—never by need, by the wish to share, or by altru-
ism. Our self-understanding is so deeply affected by the
power of the metaphor that we come to believe that it is
right to compete, to win, to conquer.

## Economism and Cultural Values

Language, in other words, shapes not only thought and
action but also the interpretation of values. Freedom, justice, welfare, and happiness are values common to every
culture, but they are contested concepts in the sense that
their meaning is subject to continuous negotiation within
any culture. In a culture of economism their meanings are
rooted in economics. Our cultural conception of justice, for
instance, is distributive rather than corrective or commu-
tative. Other interpretations are possible; for instance, we
could base our view of what constitutes just distribution on
ideas of equality, or entitlement, or need. But in a culture
of economism, our choice is dictated by the logic of the
market, which distributes according to what is deserved.
Justice in the market is based on merit; merit in turn is
earned by hard work, productivity, efficiency. We implicit-
ly accept the existing distribution of income and wealth, at
a national or global level, as fair and just because it is the
outcome of the market process. An extension of the idea of
distributive justice is seen in the argument that the market
should reward in order to attract the best people and to
provide them with incentives. The incentive argument is
the one used to justify paying chief executives more than
fifty times as much as the average worker in their companies on the grounds that their company has performed
well.[24] The problem about defining justice on the basis of
market processes is that the marketplace favors the strong,
the talented, those with genetic or educational advantages.
From a consequentialist point of view, this conception of

justice is surely incompatible not only with the gospel but also with any overall definition of human welfare or happiness.

Within the logic of the market economy, welfare and happiness are defined in a very specific way. As in the case of justice, welfare is not defined with reference to distribution. Welfare economics defines maximum welfare not in terms of human well-being, not in terms of the satisfaction of human needs, but simply in terms of getting the greatest output from a given quantity of resources. Furthermore, welfare is communally defined, and the optimal position (known as the "Pareto-optimum") for a given economy is defined without any reference to who gets what, so that in terms of the economic conception of welfare gross inequality of income is just as desirable as an equal distribution. A society or economy can thus be "Pareto-optimal" and still be "perfectly disgusting" (Sen 1982:139ff.). Even if we disregard the question of distribution, we are still left with the problem posed by definitions of welfare as "more is better." As we have come to realize in rich societies, wealth and welfare are not the same thing, although we continue to pretend that they are. Welfare cannot be measured only in terms of the economic. It also depends on the "sphere of unmeasurable social wealth" (de Romana 1989:81), on nonmonetary production, on social and cultural relationships and activities, and on the whole fabric of daily lived experience.

Economism's conception of freedom is equally narrow. Freedom is interpreted by economics as freedom from restraint in the market and freedom to choose. But we are not free to choose if we do not have the money to exercise our choice, if we do not have the knowledge to judge the merits of what is on offer, and if we do not have the time to enjoy what we buy. Also, real economic freedom is defined as much by the capability to benefit by commodities as by the possibility of acquiring them (Sen 1984). This capability will depend not only on the person; it will also depend on the context and on the environment in which the good is used. Cars give little satisfaction if roads are so congested as to discourage their use. The idea of freedom to choose and compete in the market has a hollow ring to it if its exercise restrains the freedom of others. In terms of the culture of economism, the value of "freedom for all" becomes "freedom for me at your expense."

## Conclusion

In order to gain a perspective on the cultural context to be addressed by Christian mission, we have chosen to characterize Western culture as a culture of economism. This is a systems approach to cultural description; it is holistic rather than analytical. It is designed to give a feel for the essence of the culture, to create an ethos, a cultural vision (Bateson 1958). We believe economism to be the clearest and most identifiable cultural influence on the worldviews, the meanings and the values, that serve to shape our ways of thinking and of living, but we also believe that it is the interpretation of Western culture that holds the key to understanding the problems faced by Christian mission to that culture. The next two chapters are devoted to explaining this perspective.

# 2

# Culture's Consequences

Economism is not merely the "ethos" of Western culture; it has also become the dominant cultural perspective of a world whose dimensions have shrunk to that of a "global village." It has been carried to the four corners of the globe by the institutions of Western culture—not only by bureaucratic and technocratic organizations, but also by the markets that, thanks to the power of modern communications and the force of modern technology, now form the backbone of the global economic order. In order to explore the processes that have given rise to this cultural hegemony, we need to consider the dynamics of cultural process. This in turn requires the development of a view on cultural movement and change. The idea of a process or rhythm of cultural change is not new; it has been reflected on and expressed in different ways by thinkers throughout the ages. What all their views appear to have in common is a conception of two poles between which culture moves or fluctuates. Heraclitus saw the world order as a fire alternately kindling and going out. Hegel saw human history as a spiral moving between poles of unity and disunity, that would reintegrate at a higher plane of unity. Herbert Spencer saw the universe moving "from an indefinite, incoherent homogeneity to a definite coherent heterogeneity through successive integrations and differentiations" (Toynbee 1988:89).[1]

It is this view of cultural process as alternating between the poles of integration and differentiation that we find most helpful. We see cultures as cognitive systems (Argyris and Schon 1978), complex assemblages of interrelated parts, that operate by structuring and sharing information.[2] Culture is not static; dynamic it is continually adapting and changing as information transfer gives rise to a constant process of feedback and self-correction.[3] The dimensions of this process, as well as the direction of change, will vary because of the ways in which people interact and also because of the ways in which they learn. Learning changes people, and their responses to others will change in consequence. Sometimes the effects of those changes will correct irregularities and aberrations so that the system will remain stable within existing parameters, but sometimes small changes can ramify through the cultural system so that it gradually modifies. Alternatively, small changes can have the effect of sending the system into "runaway" so that the parameters dissolve and the cultural system disintegrates. Geoffrey Bateson described this phenomenon in terms of a "growing split in the structure of ideas" that would produce eventual cultural disintegration—a phenomenon he termed "schismogenesis" (Bateson 1972).[4]

Underlying the idea of cultures as dynamic communicative and adaptive systems is the notion of purpose. Cultures are ways of life that have to provide comprehensive and coherent answers to the problems of existence. As such they are not merely systems of thought; they are also sets of values that reflect purpose and shape the meaningfulness of experience within that culture. Values will differ; they will also compete and conflict as they reflect the richness of cultural diversity. Thus, one of the basic tasks of cultural process is the management of value difference. Holding that balance between opposing values presents dilemmas that we can liken to the problem faced by the mythical helmsman who had to steer between the rock of Scylla and the whirlpool of Charybdis (Hampden-Turner 1994). The cultural helmsman must avoid conflict without inviting compromise, no single value must be allowed to dominate, and opposing cultural values must be held in creative tension in such a way that they enhance each other and work together synergically.[5]

The most basic of the value dilemmas, in the sense that it is the most important for cultural survival and identity, is that of integration and differentiation. Integration holds the culture together, but differentiation ensures the cultural variety necessary for cultures to innovate and hence evolve. Cultural change thus presents a constant pattern of differentiation and integration analogous to the pattern inherent in the structure of life itself. All physical life is the consequence of a process whereby differentiation and integration enhance each other: higher forms of life contain greater differentiation and demand greater integration than lower or less complex forms of life. But, as is the case with all life, cultural differentiation and integration must happen as a harmonious process that demonstrates balance as opposing values are held in tension. If this is the case, differentiation and integration will be synergic in the sense that they will enhance one another. Integration will draw on the richness of diversity; differentiation will be encouraged and affirmed by cultural coherence. Cultures that demonstrate this pattern will develop and grow dynamically as "virtuous circles" driven forward by cultural learning (Hampden-Turner 1994): they will be symbolic because they will be life giving, creative, and healing.

But it may also be the case that integration and differentiation are not held in balance, and that one or the other predominates. The situation will then be unstable because the mutually constraining influence of the values-in-tension is lost and the system will "run away," that is, become "schismogenetic." An integration that destroys differentiation will kill in the same way that cancer works by trying to reform all other cells to its own image; it is also the case that differentiation without integration is the basis of disintegration and entropy. Life depends on the synergy, on the working together of the different value poles. Any integration that eliminates the "different" eliminates the possibility of that synergy and has to rely on diabolic force and violence to keep the parts together.

The power of this conceptual framework becomes apparent when we apply it to our own cultural context. In the culture of economism, integration and differentiation are not held in balance. There is no doubting the integrative power of the culture, but integration is only one of the horns of a fundamental dilemma, and if it is pursued unilaterally it will produce runaway excesses. The thesis here is that the integration achieved by the culture of economism has done just this. Historically, it has manifested itself as a diabolic process sustained by structural violence at the cost of a terrifying level of cultural disintegration. In its drive toward integration, economism has ridden roughshod over the individual and over the cultural differences that constitute the richness of humanity. We see this as happening at four different levels: at the socioeconomic level, the cultural level, the political level, and the gender level. At each of these levels the fundamental dilemma between integration and differentiation manifests itself in a different way: at each level the culture of economism has served to suppress diversity, marginalizing and dehumanizing all those affected by the process. The integrative power of economism is centered largely in the institutions of that culture and in the technology they embody.[6] The institutional basis of cultural integration facilitates a concentration of power that divides the world into "oppressors" and "oppressed" at each of these four levels. We do not suggest that this thirsting for power is new. The distinction between oppressors and oppressed has always existed. What is new is the scale and the force of that power— explained by, among other things, the alliance between the culture of economism and the industrial-military complex (Lens 1970). This alliance ensures that those who reap the benefits of economism have at their disposal the means of permanently maintaining oppression at a global level.

### Globalization and the Disabling of Independent Socioeconomic Systems: The Global/Local Dilemma

*Globalization* is the term generally used to refer to the socioeconomic integration of our world. Globalization is not a new phenomenon (it used to be called "empire building"), and it has its roots in the spread of Western influence across the world three centuries ago. But it received its major impetus from nineteenth-century colonialism, which provided the food, raw materials, and minerals necessary to fuel the economic development of the West. This often involved straight expropriation, but it also involved instituting fundamental changes in modes of production— for instance, the growing of cash crops on large plantations or the setting up of "concession companies" that had the monopoly of certain types of production over a large area.[7]

Colonialism provides an excellent example of the way in which an integration realized at the cost of differentiation needs to be supported by the systematic use of structural violence. The consequences are with us today and are seen particularly in the inability of African countries to achieve economic and political stability. The worst of these consequences for the peoples of many parts of the world is that they were forced to abandon socioeconomic systems that had for centuries proved capable of ensuring their survival in favor of an economic system that, even if it provides some short-term benefits to a privileged part of the population, endangers the very survival of the people in the longer term. Existing know-how has been rendered obsolete, forgotten, and lost. Production processes have been separated from land values, the land from people, and ultimately, economic values from personal values (Hawken 1993:11). In recent decades, agribusiness has undermined traditional modes of food production. Many countries are dependent on just one or two cash crops, and the prices of these fluctuate with market conditions, which means that countries' foreign currency earnings also fluctuate. Famine has become endemic in countries that are major agricultural producers. Most African countries are net importers of food; but stagnant prices for their cash crops, rising populations, and a lack of foreign currency to buy fertilizers and agricultural machinery have meant that they cannot feed their people. Local subsistence systems are destroyed.

The role of the political powers as carriers of globalization has dwindled in importance as their place has been taken by transnational corporations. Globalization refers nowadays to the set of factors that have enabled and encouraged the spread of worldwide corporate activity over the last fifty years. Factors such as improved telecommunications, product and technology standardization, and financial liberalization have been major influences on companies' decisions to seek new markets by relocating production in other countries. Relocation, whether by building plants or acquiring foreign companies, means that transnational corporations can exploit economies of scale, use cheap labor, and adapt their products to indigenous tastes. Transnational companies have integrated their production and administrative systems worldwide so as to create a new international division of labor. On the face of it, this may appear to represent a redistribution of job opportunities to poorer countries. In fact, it increases the potential for exploitation in those countries, a process that is often made possible by the cooperation of local groups who gain wealth and power in exchange.

Globalization is a juggernaut (Steingard and Fitzgibbon 1995) in the sense that it is a cumulative process. Whereas the world economy grows at an annual rate of 2–3 percent, transnational corporate activity grows at 8–10 percent per annum. Global corporations in spite of their size, are accountable to no authority; the annual turnover of the largest companies is frequently greater than the gross national product of the host country.[8] They take advantage of global differences in labor and safety legislation to ensure that labor-intensive processes can be located in countries where the absence of unions and the existence of repressive regimes permit long hours, low pay, and the use of child labor. "Dirty" or dangerous processes can be done in countries where governments are not environmentally sensitive. Companies have considerable bargaining power with governments that want employment opportunities for their people, and with elites who hope for personal gain. This fact also allows companies to evade national taxation by "transfer-pricing" intracompany cross-border transactions so that profits show only in those countries with low rates of company taxation.

One of the myths of globalization is that it brings prosperity to person and planet (Steingard and Fitzgibbon 1995). Even a cursory glance at the realities of global capitalism reveals a different story. The major consequence of the process of globalization is the absolute poverty of over a fifth of humanity at world level and the deepening of differentials everywhere. Even in the rich countries of the West, there is increasing structural poverty because of the unemployment that has become endemic in Europe and to a lesser extent in the United States.[9] One-quarter of all households in the United Kingdom are now on some form of state assistance. People can no longer work because the opportunity to do so is not available. New technologies have reduced the number of working hours necessary to maintain a given level of production. Giant companies

source labor-intensive and even knowledge-intensive production abroad, and small businesses do not create suffi-
cient employment to compensate. There is an increasing
move toward short-time and part-time work as companies
attempt to reduce costs in the drive toward greater profits.
The result is that even among the employed we are seeing
a new poverty and increasing insecurity. In fact, what the
rich countries are experiencing is a phenomenon that has
existed for a long time in Third World countries—the dual-
ization of the economy, where a modern technological
sector providing jobs and high incomes coexists with a
precarious, low-wage, low-income sector.[10] The social consequences of this are now becoming obvious: the growth of
the 1980s produced higher levels of apprehension, violence, dislocation, and environmental degradation,
because in the United States, for instance, three-quarters
of the income increase went to the richest 1 per cent
(Hawken 1993:17).

The costs of structural unemployment are enormous.
United States workers made redundant by the closure of
manufacturing plants become a burden to the taxpayers
through the need for social support payments. This
increases the budget deficit, making free-market expansionism even more vital to U.S. economic survival. As well
as costs associated with reduced output, which make countries less able to care for their needy, there are the costs of
misdirected education and wasted training, the increased
demand on the social and health services, and increased
crime, vandalism, and social dislocation. But above all
there are the personal costs. In a consumer society, where
social status is directly related to employment, being out of
work hurts not only the pocket but also the self-esteem of
those who believed themselves to be good employees. But
more deeply than that, the lack of opportunity to work
means that people are denied the possibility of realizing
their own humanity, their own potential (John Paul II

1984:20). Young people in particular cannot take responsibility for their own future and that of the community. The culture of economism does not recognize this problem; it treats work as something objective, sold to the employer. People are simply instruments of production, at the service of the interests of capital. There is something profoundly wrong with a system that so obviously neglects the interests of so many to serve the interests of the few.

Globalization is the visible manifestation of the obsessive drive for economic growth—for more resources, more markets, more products. The dominant belief that all inequalities can be resolved by faster rates of expansion has permitted the institutions of economism to expand their world presence to an extent unparalleled by any other imperial thrust. The institutions of global capitalism plunder the ecosystem: they consume energy, they use nonrenewable raw materials, they create toxic waste. The diabolic consequences are there for all to see: the environmental degradation, the threat to biodiversity, and the pollution that is now threatening life on the planet. It took ten thousand days to create the energy burned in one day by our present world economy. At the present rate of extinction, we are set to lose 20 percent of all species within the next 20–40 years. We have lost 17 percent of the arable land in the world since World War II. The capacity of our world system to "carry" the burdens imposed by the drive for growth is being systematically exceeded, but the burdens fall unevenly across countries. Tropical rain forests are razed in Brazil to grow soybeans that are fed to German cows so that they can produce surplus butter and cheese for storing in refrigerators. The cost of those surpluses is the displacement of a million forest settlers who now live in urban slums. However, the litany of disaster will not continue indefinitely, because it is estimated that should world growth be such as to double the standard of living within the next forty years, we will have mathematically exceeded the capacity of the planet to sustain us. The myth, so central to economism, of "growth without limits" has led us to regard as progress the destruction of the earth's capacity to support life.[11]

Globalization is now a permanent fact of our existence. But as a world, we need to find ways of redressing its integrative excesses, of recovering the balance between the benefits of global integration and the advantages of local economic diversity. In order to do this we need to identify new forms of socioeconomic differentiation that can coexist synergically with an integrated and sustainable world economy. But production is not the only issue; we also need to ensure that consumers worldwide are not brainwashed into believing that their identity, social status, and self-worth are dependent on their consumption of global products, and that they have a chance to discover that their needs can be met equally well by products produced on a smaller scale.

### The Universalism of Economism and the Undermining of Particular Cultures: The Unity/Diversity Dilemma

Economism as a world culture claims universal legitimacy. The universalism of this claim lies at the basis of a modernity grounded in a belief in the perfectibility of social organization. There is therefore an implicit assumption that other cultures should also be brought to share in that "progress" by undergoing a process of modernization. The "modernization" of traditional cultures is done by "developing" the "backward" traditional cultures in the "underdeveloped" world. This is achieved by progressively introducing a "modern sector" linked to the world economy, which, it is hoped, will transform and progressively replace the whole of the traditional way of life. In this way, so the myth of development tells us, traditional societies can break free from the narrow confines of their particular prescientific cultures that condemn them to poverty and superstition, and can share in the benefits of modernity with its promise of science, advanced technology, health, and wealth.

The assumption that this process represents an improvement in the human condition rests on a belief in the universal validity of so-called scientific knowledge and its absolute superiority over "prescientific" worldviews. Because it operates with a simplistic, objectivist understanding of human knowledge, the culture of economism marginalizes prescientific wisdom as an obstacle to modernity and hence undermines any culture with which it enters into contact. Indigenous cultures are sterilized and silenced. Peoples are uprooted from the worldviews, symbolic systems, institutions, and rituals that organize their existence and provide answers to their quest for meaning and purpose. These peoples, whose cultural frameworks are sacrificed on the altar of modernization, are the same peoples who form the mass of the "have-nots" in the world. The process of development gives these people only the minimum level of education needed to serve the alien and alienating interests of the "haves," who monopolize the information and knowledge networks that are the main tools of the dominant culture of economism.

Cultural homogenization has ensured for a significant part of humanity the loss of traditional wisdom, technology, and knowledge, without replacing them with access to the technologies and information networks of the rich. Lost with those cultures has been the diversity in ways of being human—languages, crafts, family structures, traditional ways of healing and nourishment. Within the next decade, California will lose thirty-four Native American languages that have existed for over a thousand years (Hawken 1993). In Australia, mining has desecrated the lands inhabited by the spirits of Aboriginal ancestors. In Africa, whole nations have disappeared, and with them unique and irrecoverable ways of being human. The environment and culture of the Ogoni people of Southern Nigeria have been

destroyed, with the collusion of their own repressive government, in the search for oil. The exploitation of land and
resources in South America has dispersed the peoples
whose cultures depended on those habitats.

Cultural impoverishment has happened not only in the
poor countries of the world, but also in the interior of the
rich countries themselves. The division of labor created by
industrialization has turned people into specialists skilled
at doing one job only. As knowledge-intensive systems
come to dominate society, vernacular knowledge disap-
pears (de Romana 1989). People no longer know how to
repair, to build, to cook traditional meals, to grow vegeta-
bles. They cannot identify trees, birds, or plants. The lack
of breadth in their perception of the world around them
impoverishes their ability to imagine, to express, to create.
They lose the capacity to judge because they no longer
have a sense of the fundamental human priorities.
Surrounded by computers and with access to the most
sophisticated information networks, people find themselves unable to answer the most basic fundamental question about the meaning of human existence.

One of the most noticeable effects of the culture of
economism is the accelerated pace of living. Work has
become the dominant organizing principle of existence in
a way that represents a uniquely new human experience.
In fact, the way we live suggests that we are addicted to the
pressure and the stress as a way to prevent ourselves from
feeling or from knowing ourselves (Hawken 1993:124). Our
lives enact the self-fulfilling assumption of modern economic culture—the cultural fact of a scarcity that exists
because wants are limitless. We are conditioned to believe
that we can never have enough. The drive to accumulate
and to consume reduces leisure time and increases the
pressure to perform and to achieve. Leisure itself becomes
a commodity to be consumed, but because time is scarce,
leisure activities have a time factor attached to them. The

aim is to get the most enjoyment in the least time; therefore it is important to be "doing" something after work or
on weekends. The consequence is that people have little
time for making community or for enjoying each other's
company. The lack of community creates a vacuum for
those without close personal ties; material wealth is of little human significance to those who live with loneliness,
alienation, and despair. In fact, the culture of economism
becomes a radically impoverished culture incapable of ful-
filling the most fundamental human aspirations. We lose a
life-enhancing vernacular realm, and we incur life-impov-
erishing social costs (de Romana 1989:83).

The integrative process of creating one worldview and
one way of life is fostered by monopolistically controlled
media loaded with the "values" of economism. "News" is
syndicated worldwide by a very few news agencies. The
battle for control of global telecasting is fought by businesses interested only in the commercial aspects of global
television. Reality is rearranged by advertising, which creates a symbiosis between commodity characteristics and
peoples' fears, hopes, and desires, thus ensuring that the
deepest emotions are linked to the need to consume.
Reality is also rearranged by the invasion of our lives by
television, by the importation into our living rooms of war,
famine, and violence. How can human suffering be of any
real significance when it is possible to watch children
starve while we eat our supper?

Cultures forge a people's deeply felt identity, and when
that identity is threatened the risk is that people will react
violently to that threat. Aggressive universalism produces
its own opposing excesses—nationalism, tribalism, and
radical fundamentalism. All these excesses are on the
increase (Kaplan 1994). The violent confrontations that
happen as a result provide a justification for the further
"arming" of the dominant culture in order to maintain its
position. Here we have yet another example of a structural

violence that needs to use force to protect the monopoly of access to knowledge and to the power that goes with it.

Ultimately, universalism is a form of integration that carries in itself the seed of its own failure. The challenge we face as a world is to find a form of cultural integration that will neutralize the sectarian, exclusivistic, and divisive tendencies and temptations of particular cultures, while at the same time respecting and enhancing the variety and richness of cultural alternatives.

### Economism as an Authoritarian Threat to Freedom and Participation: The Authority/Freedom Dilemma

The integrative tendencies of the culture of economism that exist at the socioeconomic and cultural levels are even more marked at the political level. Prior to colonialism, the world was composed of a myriad of loosely linked political units, which only occasionally attempted to extend their control over neighboring units. The colonial enterprise, driven by economic motivation, effected radical political integration of many of those units by removing political control from them and centralizing administrative and political power. Africa serves as a wonderful illustration of this drive to integrate. As a consequence of the Berlin pact at the end of the nineteenth century, a mosaic of roughly two thousand ethnic units was reduced to half a dozen colonial blocs controlled from the colonial capitals. It is therefore not surprising that the political independence granted in the sixties to a series of artificially created nation-states has not resulted in a corresponding economic and cultural independence, for it has merely imposed yet another integrative process on disparate peoples.

The shift of power in the West toward the United States, the growth of Japan, the autarky of China, and finally the disintegration of the Soviet bloc and the growth of the European Union leave us with a world where the destiny of the whole of humanity rests in very few hands. It is clear that the power centers of our world coincide with the dominant economic blocs; continental China will become the largest world economy in absolute terms in a few years time. What is also evident is that the political ideologies of the people governing those blocs become increasingly irrelevant, because it is the so-called market economy, and the assumptions and goals of the culture of economism as carried in its institutions, that controls politics everywhere. The suspicion that political ideologies are becoming irrelevant because politics is being reduced to "following the laws of the market" is currently creating growing political unease in a number of leading democratic countries. The scandals and government crises in countries like Italy, Spain, Belgium, France, and even Great Britain are radically undermining the confidence of peoples in their own governments. What emerges from these crises is the conviction that politicians no longer aim to serve the interests of their constituents, but rather the interests of powerful socioeconomic groups, and their own interests in consequence. This conviction is accompanied by the realization that today's politicians are devoid of real power, because political power resides with those who wield economic power, and that public servants everywhere serve private money interests rather than the interests of those whose taxes pay their salaries.

The Spanish people, who have always mistrusted their governments of any kind and any color, attribute the formal power of politicians and governments to what they call *poderes fácticos*—the real power—which operates hidden behind the backs of politicians and manipulates their attitudes and actions. Democracy, the people's participation in the ordering of their own life, is perceived as a meaningless facade that hides the ruthless authoritarianism of corporate self-interest. Hawken's analysis of the political life of the United States confirms the worst Spanish suspicions:

Money now creates the milieu in which debates are framed, voices heard, decisions made. Corporations have created a multi-billion (dollar) industry of lobbyists, public relation firms, scholarly papers prepared by conservative think tanks, artificially generated "people's" campaigns, "expert" witnesses at public hearings who work for, or are paid by, corporate interests, and lawyers based in Washington, D.C., whose sole purpose is to influence lawmakers and regulators in their offices, in four-star restaurants, at lavish receptions, on overseas junkets…. It is in these privileged and cloistered domains, and not on the floor of the Senate and the House, that the decisions of our government are made (Hawken 1993:109).

There is in consequence an enormous accumulation of power vested in people who do not represent peoples' interests, are not democratically elected and are not accountable, and who shape behind the scenes the laws that allow them to amass and protect their accumulated power. In the extreme case, the culture of economism leads ultimately to a form of totalitarianism, where the only thing demanded from all political institutions is not to interfere with the "free working of the market"—a euphemism for the free wheeling and dealing of the money oligarchy that dominates the world economy and makes a charade of democratic institutions. Even in our own backyard, "one percent of American society owns nearly 60 percent of corporate equities and about 40 percent of the total wealth of this nation. These are the plutocrats who wield the power" (Hawken 1993:111). The same pattern is found in most countries of the world and becomes even more apparent in the poorest countries, where a handful of individuals control a huge proportion of those countries' limited wealth. It is therefore not surprising that the promise of support to the poor countries of the world by

Western countries is made conditional on the setting up of democratic institutions and on a commitment to the free-market economy. Countries who are prepared to open their frontiers to the free working of the market are helped by the West without too close an examination of their democratic credentials, as the recent history of Ghana demonstrates.

Economic monopoly cultural monopoly and political monopoly coalesce in the same exclusive club of corporate power. This group is beyond politics and ready to collaborate with any political system so long as the system accepts its rules of the game and is ready to assume its cultural forms. The transformation of China's economy into a market economy is a case in point. This power center relies on its structural links with the military industrial complex to keep at bay all the threats to its freedoms and to the institutions that enable it to operate (Lens 1970). The political integration of the world in which we live has produced an authoritarian world where most of humanity has lost the freedom to participate in the shaping of its own destiny. In addition to being economically marginalized and culturally impoverished, most of humanity is also politically disenfranchised.

### Economism and Male Domination: The Masculine/Feminine Dilemma

Western culture, together with most other cultures, is based on a patriarchy that is deeply embedded in all its cultural systems—philosophical, political, and social. In these cultures, "men—by force, direct pressure, or through ritual, tradition, law and language, customs, etiquette, education, and the division of labor—determine what part women shall or shall not play, and... the female is everywhere subsumed under the male" (Rich 1977:32). Patriarchy has always been taken for granted and has influenced all our ideas about nature and about our relation to the universe.

By the simple use of the word *mankind* we establish a worldview that makes half of humanity invisible.

If there is any justification for patriarchy, it must be that there are fundamental differences between the sexes—differences that make women in some sense inferior. There are indeed masculine and feminine characteristics, recognized from the earliest times in Chinese culture as "yin" and "yang." But the Chinese believed that each one of us embodies both masculine and feminine characteristics, and biological research confirms this intuition. This view of human nature is not that of our patriarchal culture, which has established a social order in which all men are supposed to be masculine—that is, possess only "yang" characteristics—and all women are supposed to be feminine. Little boys play with trucks and guns, little girls with Barbie dolls. Active men can then "naturally" dominate passive women.

The culture of economism is a paradigm of everything masculine. It produces an integration of society at the cost of the oppression not only of women, but, more radically, of the feminine in us all. The culture of economism expresses all the excesses of one-sided masculine characteristics and values. It is aggressive, competitive, and manipulative; it is hierarchical and totally preoccupied with power and control; it has a rational, analytical, "scientific" orientation; it sets humankind as conqueror and exploiter of nature. In order to live comfortably, or successfully, within this culture, we are required to be people, men or women, who are prepared to demonstrate our competitive spirit, our aggression, our ability to control, our need to dominate. We must suppress our gentleness, our intuition, our ability to cooperate, our need to nurture.

The most recent project of Western patriarchy has been the drive for development. As a continuation of the process of colonialization, development has exploited and excluded women as it has exploited nature and eroded cultures. Women's participation in the development process has been asymmetric; they have borne the costs but have been excluded from the benefits. Research done in connection with the UN Decade for Women concluded that "with a few exceptions, women's relative access to economic resources, incomes and employment has worsened, their burden of work has increased, and their relative and even absolute health, nutritional and educational status has declined" (Shiva 1989:3). Women suffered particularly from the loss of land rights, from the expansion of cash crops, and from the ecological destruction that deprived them of the resources on which their existence as sustainers of society was based. The bias of Western economism against diversity, against nature, and against women has destroyed traditional complementarities of male and female work roles, and led to a maldevelopment that "violates the integrity of organic, interconnected and interdependent systems, that sets in motion a process of exploitation, inequality, injustice and violence" (Shiva 1989:7).

The masculine, aggressive approach to reality is at the root of the violence that we have identified as existing at every level of our world system. It is also the root of another aspect of the negative consequences of the culture of economism—the ruthless and shortsighted exploitation of the earth's resources for short-term profit. This system is unsustainable for two reasons: first because of the spiraling costs of the structural violence needed to keep the oppressed in their place; and second because the rapid destruction of nonrenewable resources and of the resource base itself is endangering the future viability of the human race. It is a measure of the "masculine" arrogance of the culture that we blind ourselves to these facts.

## Conclusion

Possibilities of integration and differentiation represent two horns of a cultural dilemma. If these opposing values are held in balance, the two sides of the dilemma enhance each other; they will be symbolic, spontaneously cooperating and trusting each other. The result is life-enhancing synergy and harmonious growth. Our analysis of the way the culture of economism attempts to integrate humanity into one socioeconomic system at the cost of differentiation suggests that we are in the presence of a diabolic, schismogenetic, vicious circle, where the suppression of differences has increasingly to be achieved by the use of institutionalized violence at a cost of enormous suffering and of danger to survival (Fig. 1). This integration defeats its own purpose, because it is achieved only at the cost of painful structural disintegration; furthermore, it is clearly unsustainable. The culture of economism is in a real sense a culture of death, because it has no imaginable acceptable future.

What is very strange is that those who benefit from the culture of economism fail to see that it carries the seeds of its own destruction. There seems to be a kind of mental and physical "apartheid" that shields us all from the reality and the extent of oppression and injustice endemic in the system. It is strange, too, that the notion of moral responsibility for the marginalization, poverty, and powerlessness of so many plays so little part in public debate. Perhaps we avoid that issue by holding to the belief that the workings of the economy are mechanistic and therefore beyond the realm of morality. We certainly operate a kind of "transference syndrome" by passing the responsibility for their own condition to those who are at the receiving end of the integrative nature of the culture. And if we do suffer pangs of conscience, we assuage them by "charity" to the poor, and by "aid" as comforting and comfortable compassion (Elliott 1987:34).

Fig. 1

**ECONOMISM**

| VALUE EXCESSES (CONSEQUENCES) | DIFFERENTIATING VALUES | 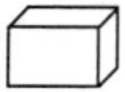 | INTEGRATIVE VALUES | VALUE EXCESSES (CAUSES) |
|---|---|---|---|---|
| destruction of alternative economic systems **leading to** poverty, social unrest | **local** | S Y | **global** | growth, accumulation, globalization |
| destruction of cultural diversity **leading to** nationalism fundamentalism | **diversity** | N E | **unity** | universalism, destruction of cultural diversity, global consumerism |
| marginalization from political participation **leading to** revolution | **freedom** | R G | **authority** | market power, corporate power, economic hegemony |
| marginalization of women, **leading to** radical feminism | **feminine** | Y | **masculine** | patriarchy male domination |
| **OPPRESSED POWERLESS** | **DISINTEGRATION** | | **STRUCTURAL VIOLENCE POWERFUL** | **OPPRESSORS** |

# 3

# The Church and Economism

There is a close relationship between the church and the culture of economism. The very origins of Western culture are to be found in Christianity, which together with western philosophical traditions was for centuries the major influence on its cultural value systems. It is also true that Christianity gained the benefits of its status as a world religion largely because of the growing influence of the West. Christianity welcomed the opportunities for the expansion of its universalist mission offered by colonial expansion.

But the church's spectacular growth during the last 150 years, particularly in Africa, has to be set against the dramatic decline of its influence in the prosperous countries of the West. The process of secularization and the defensive attitude of most churches toward the Enlightenment resulted in the progressive marginalization of Christianity not only in the sphere of public life, but in terms of its influence on the value systems and behavior of its own followers. Within the Roman Catholic Church the profound crisis of many communities in the West contrasts starkly with the continuous vitality of the church in other parts of the world. The minority in the West who are still practicing Christians experience the fact that their daily life is fundamentally shaped not by Christianity but by the cultural influence of economism, and that only for an hour a week do they remember that they are something more than consumers driven by self-interest. Their weekly visit to church may inspire them and give them personal hope and meaning, but it has little effect on their working lives or on their lives as citizens, where they often feel alienated and powerless.[1]

The fact is that the Christian communities in the West have lost not only their enthusiasm but also their missionary drive. The recruitment to the ordained ministry is falling to dangerously low levels; the average age of the clergy is rising continually, and missionaries no longer come from Western countries. Mission has ceased to become unidirectional and is becoming multidirectional. We even joke that we are forming missionaries in the non-Western world so that we can send them to re-evangelize the de-Christianized West. The real truth is that the Western church finds itself incapable of making the gospel relevant to a Western world shaped by secularism and its culture of economism.

Our contention here is simple: it is that the inability of Christian mission to address the challenge posed by the culture of economism can be explained by the fact that the church and the culture of economism are completely symbiotic. The institutions of the mainstream churches in the West have allied themselves over the centuries with the culture of economism and bear a large share of the responsibility for the problems that it has created. Christianity has not only provided the culture of economism with its fundamental perceptions, attitudes, and structures; it has also accommodated to that culture in a very fundamental way. The acculturation of the church to the dominant culture emasculates gospel values, and in consequence the gospel loses its radicalism and its capacity to direct the transformation of the society's culture.

In order to be able to be part of the solution, the church has to recognize that it is part of the problem. We consider this recognition essential. It is the starting point for the church's own attempt at transformation and conversion, and for the recovery of gospel values that is necessary in order to recreate a healthy tension between the church and the dominant culture. The church must "de-link," must distance itself from the culture of economism in order to be able to call it to conversion. It is the call "Convert, because the Kingdom of God is near at hand" that is the essence of mission. An accommodated, acculturated church cannot make that call.

## Christianity as the Architect of the Culture of Economism

The acculturation of the Christian church in the West goes back a very long way. It can be characterized most accurately as the accommodation of Christianity to power. With the Constantinian Settlement,[2] Christianity was seduced by the advantages gained from the protection of the secular institutions and became blinded to the diabolic side of power.[3] Because of the symbiotic relationship between church and secular power structures, secular and religious government institutions came increasingly to mirror each other. As institutions in secular society emerged, the church became not only feudal and monarchic, it also became the world's first hierarchical bureaucratic organization. And when inherited and aristocratic power was progressively replaced by the power of accumulated wealth, the church had no difficulty broadening its collaboration with the secular powers by allying itself with the interests of the wealthy class that was financing its various enterprises. As a counterpart to this collaboration and as a reward for the blessing and defense of the social status quo, the church was able to use the colonial ventures of Christian powers to expand its own influence. We see this particularly in the conquest and evangelization of America. The alliance between the church and the secular powers was occasionally challenged, but the efforts of, for instance, the Franciscan movement and the Radical Reformation did not succeed in weakening the links between the main Catholic and Protestant churches and the secular institutions.

The Enlightenment and its attendant revolutions (political, social, and scientific) broke the structural link between the religious and the secular by disengaging the secular institutions of society (state, business, science, philosophy, and education) from the tutelage of the churches, which were then progressively pushed out of public life into the private realm.[4] However, the independence of the secular did not destroy the reliance of the churches on the institutions of power. The different churches again used the colonial expansion of the Western countries as a vehicle for their own expansion without so much as a word of condemnation for the colonial enterprise in general. But while the churches were using their energy happily growing in the territories opened to them by colonization, they failed to realize that in their own Western backyard an alternative culture was emerging that was to claim the adherence of church members, body and soul, by its promises of instant success and gratification, and of the elimination of all evils afflicting humanity. Science and the invisible hand of the market would gradually replace God and God's providence in the hearts of believers. The culture of economism can be compared to a sucker in the Christian tree that grew at the expense of the tree itself; like all suckers, it owed its justification and its most fundamental assumptions to the mother tree—in this case Christianity. Unfortunately, what it absorbed were the more ambiguous characteristics of historic Christianity: its exclusivism, aggressiveness, and superiority complex; its perceived God-given right to conquer; its dogmatism; its individualism; and its hierarchical behavior.

The dominating, manipulative, and aggressive character of economism cannot be fully understood unless one understands the role played by Christianity in the development of the root understandings in the culture of economism. It was the certainty of Christianity's possession of a monopoly of truth and salvation, together with its sense of universal mission understood as a fight against evil, that together underpinned the myth of scientific truth as ultimate objective truth. This is the conviction that engendered universal support for the colonial expansion of the West as a civilizing duty. It was the backdrop of the fight against evil that was to create a culture of conquest, competition, and success. It was the hierarchical and authoritarian understanding of the exercise of power in the church that provided the most fundamental model for the organization of business corporations. It was the superiority of man over creation and the command to subdue the earth that created in the West the mentality that legitimated the exploitation of people and resources so characteristic of the Industrial Revolution. And it is Eve's responsibility for introducing suffering in the world that continues to justify the domination of women in Christianity and in the cultures that Christianity shapes.

At the root of all that, there is an exclusivism that is one of the most fundamental corruptions of the heart of the gospel, an exclusivism translated as aggressiveness toward anyone "other." A gospel that was originally about "a God who loves all" became through successive traumatic events a gospel that preached that "God loves only good and faithful members of the church." As Christians we have to admit that this exclusivism has been a characteristic of all Christian churches and communities until very recently, and that it has been the source of intolerance and cruelty among Christians and by Christians toward non-Christians. It was this intolerance that motivated the search for a secular nonreligious basis on which to build society in a Europe devastated by religious wars. Unfortunately, the resultant secular society inherited the exclusivism and the aggressive superiority complex that was at the heart of the problem. The sense of superiority was reinforced by the fact that the scientific and industrial revolutions actually allowed a secular West and its individualistic entrepreneurs, driven as they were by a Puritan sense of mission and purpose, to begin to believe in the possibility of whole-world domination. The newer developments in information and communications have made that possibility a reality. The result is a world thrown into a vortex of violent transformation. The churches find themselves rudderless in the midst of that vortex. In terms of our model, this situation represents a dangerous vicious circle where the concentration of power in the hands of a few has created a black hole that threatens to swallow the future of humanity.

## The Roman Catholic Church as the Mirror of Economism

Church and culture have each adopted the diabolic characteristics of the other. Economism owes many of its negative characteristics to Christianity, and the Roman Catholic Church mirrors economism in its failure to achieve an internal balance between cultural integration and differentiation. If we look at the pre–Vatican II ecclesial paradigm, we are struck by the parallels between the Church and the culture of economism. The Church has its own organizational "culture," with its own beliefs and values, ways of decision taking and acting, expressed in the rituals, myths, and symbols that create the meanings grounding coherence and continuity (Hofstede 1991, 1980). But in cultural terms, the Church suffers from exactly the same one-sidedness as does the culture of economism, in the sense that cultural integration is achieved at the cost of differentiation. "Espoused theory" in Church circles speaks continually of "service," whereas actual "theory in use" (Hampden-Turner 1994:74) betrays a preoccupation with power and control. Both economism and the Roman Catholic Church—at least until the rethinking of the Second Vatican Council—represent power systems that claim to use their power "for" people while in reality exercising power "over" people.[5] This similarity suggests that not only is the Church acculturated to the culture of economism, but that both suffer from similar defects in their understanding and methods of managing their cultural dilemmas. And just as in the wider culture the failure to create synergy results in excesses that brand the culture as a failure in human terms, so in the case of the Church's organizational culture the failure to steer successfully between opposing values results in a failure in the key organizational task of mission.

## The Church as a Vehicle of Globalization: The Global/Local Dilemma

Colonialism was one of the main means of global economic integration, and the missionary enterprise was undertaken in tandem with that process. The churches explicitly understood their mission as a purely religious one, but they could not avoid collaborating in the process of socioeconomic transformation carried out by the colonial powers. Colonial administrations were often happy to leave in the hands of the missionaries a great array of social services, from education to health, from vocational training to agricultural projects. All of that work was appropriate for missionaries in the sense that it belonged to the familiar category of "works of mercy" and thus counted as an expression of Christian charity.

In fact, it was the churches who frequently provided the infrastructures needed for the colonial system to work and who gave a human face to colonialism. In exchange for that collaboration, the churches gained the protection of the colonial powers and considerable freedom of action. But the hidden reality was that the institutions transplanted to colonial territories carried the values and presuppositions that underpinned the culture of economism. In most cases the churches were unaware that they were collaborating in

a process of ruthless exploitation that was progressively
disintegrating local economic systems and harnessing local
economies to the dynamics of the global economy. In many
cases missionaries did oppose and contain some local abuses,
but they were powerless to influence the far-reaching trans-
formations that were reducing colonized peoples to a
dependent and exploited socioeconomic position. The
apparent short-term gains in terms of health, education,
and modernization hid the structural problems that were
later to explode in the form of destructive vicious circles of
deprivation, social unrest, and structural violence after the
withdrawal of political colonial control and its replacement
by neocolonialism.

This pattern has been repeated during the last four
decades in the guise of the church's sponsorship of "development." Development has failed because it is part of the
aid strategy that attempts to address the consequences of
neocolonialism without touching any of the structural
mechanisms at the root of the problems. The proof is that
development aid is now largely replaced by disaster relief
aimed at ensuring bare physical survival. The engagement
of missionaries and church workers in development and
increasingly in disaster relief locks them into a relationship
that is deeply conditioned by the culture of economism.
Their relationship with those they have come to serve,
and to whom they seek to witness, becomes a power relationship of rich toward poor that reduces the relationship
to one of economic need-satisfaction. The role of the missionary becomes that of provider, and people are reduced
to the level of consumers. Even if this relationship is exercised in a benign, paternalistic way, it destroys the dignity
of the aid recipients as well as their capacity to solve their
own problems with their own traditional knowledge and
technologies. In fact, development aid, with its heavy
reliance on outside experts, capital, and technology, continues to be an agent of destruction of all traditional

socioeconomic systems. So-called appropriate technologies are often developed by the developers themselves. Very rarely is there an effort to build on existing local technology. Again, as in colonial times, the high media profile of development and disaster relief conceals the real causes of structural poverty in the Third World. And again, as in colonial times, the church has been in the forefront of a strategy that now threatens the very survival of global socioeconomic diversity.

Happy with the opportunities afforded for its own growth and expansion by colonialism and postcolonialism, the institutional church failed to see the wood for the trees. Distracted also by the threat of communism, church leaders were blind to the costs of the progressive global socioeconomic domination and integration carried out by the West. Church institutions themselves became harnessed to the culture of economism by sharing in the well being that was the consequence of the accumulation of wealth in the West. There is no doubt that the church institutions control immense collective wealth, even if that wealth is mostly administered by a relatively modest class and is genuinely used for a variety of nonprofit social services. It cannot be said that the church as an institution belongs to the corporate plutocracy that controls the world economy, but it is still true that the church institutions belong comfortably to the world of the "haves" and as such share collectively in the responsibility of the deprivation of the "have-nots" because they benefit from it even if they are mainly unwitting collaborators in the mechanics of the global integration of socioeconomic power.

### The Universalism of the Church: The Unity/Diversity Dilemma

There is a striking parallel between the emphasis on cultural integration in the pre–Vatican II ecclesial paradigm, and that in the culture of economism. The similarity is not surprising when we recall that the basis of cultural exclusivism in economism was inherited from the long history of exclusivism in Christianity, which blinded the church to the existence of any truth, goodness, or value outside Christianity. The ideal of integration is in both cases unity as uniformity—integration on the basis of one single culture at the expense of the differentiation and diversity of cultures. This is the mind-set that legitimates the understanding of mission as the implantation of church structures. The implantation model of mission is universalist; it integrates at the cost of cultural differentiation. Diversity is seen as divisive and a direct consequence of sin, whereas unity is identified with grace.[6]

It is also the mind-set that forged a common purpose between the colonial powers that saw it as their duty to civilize the savage and the primitive, and a church that had a mission to abolish superstition. In fact, it was Christianity that brought "civilization" to mission territories. The "Christian culture" that the church propagated at home and transplanted to its mission territories had acritically absorbed many of the presuppositions and conclusions of the Enlightenment and hence of the culture of economism. The missionaries brought with them not only the structures and institutions of their church, but the worldviews of scientism and historicism, notions of progress, and the individualism of Western post-Christian culture. "Becoming Christian" was a process inextricably linked to becoming European; it required a shedding of traditional worldviews and ways of living, and ultimately a total rupture with peoples' cultural roots.

The churches offered remedies to the problems of the peoples they aimed to evangelize, but they understood those problems not as the people experience them but as the missionaries saw them. Their understanding was—and still is—conditioned by a reductionistic scientific worldview with its mechanistic understanding of the world. The most obvious example of this myopic view of reality is the treatment of sickness. Confronted in many mission territories with appalling levels of endemic sickness, the missionaries answered the crying needs of the people by introducing modern scientific medicine. Modern medicine offered mechanistic help in case of sickness; at the same time, it neglected completely the complex world of feeling and emotions that the reality of sickness awakened in the people—feelings and emotions that were in fact addressed by the holistic practices of traditional medicine. But traditional medicine operated in the context of a worldview totally neglected and despised by the missionaries. The fact that missionaries lacked any understanding of these worldviews meant that missionary activity completely failed to reach and evangelize the core realities of people's lives— their fears, their feelings, their emotions, and their hopes.

That kind of cultural schizophrenia exists everywhere. People—in Africa, for instance become Christian for the many benefits (spiritual, social, and material) that church membership brings, but a whole world of values, myths, beliefs, feelings, concerns, and emotions remains deeply rooted in a cultural background that has not been integrated with the church's teaching and way of life. People find themselves living in a no-man's-land between two different and nonintegrated cultural contexts, and experiencing profound levels of disease when moving from one to the other. In most cases they try to hide their feelings from the people ministering to them, because they run the risk of exposing themselves to incomprehension and ridicule. People even feel guilty when they experience the power and influence of their traditional culture in their lives. At the same time they will always feel like second-class citizens in the superimposed foreign culture. It is regrettable that the Christian church and Christian mission are in fact vehicles by which the dominant Western culture exercises hegemony in this way.

We can see therefore how the universalism of the church combines with that of the culture of economism to integrate the world at the cost of cultural differentiation. The profound unease experienced by those at the receiving end of the process creates tensions that result in schismogenesis: the visible face of this is the phenomenon of breakaway groups who resolve their cultural stress by recreating social cohesion around the worldview that is consonant with their deepest emotional identity. This is what is happening in Africa, for instance, with the continuous formation of African Independent Churches.[7]

## Clericalism in the Church:
## the Authority/Freedom Dilemma

In the culture of economism, decision taking is vested in the hands of the few. The value of freedom is sacrificed to the desire for control and to the obsession with the use of power. No great amount of imagination is needed to realize how much that description parallels the pre–Vatican II ecclesial paradigm in the Roman Catholic Church. The main difference is that, in the case of the Church, power is understood as religious and sacred rather than temporal. In the hierarchical church paradigm, the Church has the monopoly of the means of otherworldly salvation. Salvific power descends in a channel from God through Jesus Christ, founder of the church, and is vested by the Spirit in a hierarchy of ordained ministers—Pope, bishops, priests, deacons—who have sole control of the means of salvation and are hence its agents. Ministers monopolize the teaching, governing, and sanctifying functions in the Church;[8] all other members of the Church are passive recipients of the work of salvation. Moreover, in this ecclesial understanding there is an overriding concern for individual salvation achieved through reception of the sacraments. Sacramental dispensation is controlled by the clerical class, who therefore represent the sole channel by which the faithful can "get to heaven."

In view of this, it is not surprising that the main preoccupation of all the ministers is the scrupulous dispensation of the sacraments and the maintenance of the Church structures (doctrine, parishes, dioceses). At the same time, the individualism prevalent in the model penetrates the clerical structure and introduces a hierarchical way of thinking and of doing at all levels in order to assure a proper transmission of salvific power "from top to bottom." A rigidly structured and centralized authoritarian hierarchy demands absolute obedience, tight discipline, and uniform behavior of those lower down in the chain. All relationships are determined by the corresponding categories of "authority" and "obedience" and of "superior" and "inferior," and ministers tend to see themselves as individual (and lonely) links of a descending chain. The person in authority stands always "on top" and becomes a "solitary figure"—pope, bishop, parish priest.

There is another dimension to the Church's hierarchical organizational structure. The central bureaucratic structure, known as the Curia, consists of a number of administrative departments know as Congregations headed by cardinals, who are in charge of different aspects of the life of the Church. To these, after the Second Vatican Council, were added a number of Secretariats, also headed by cardinals, which were established to take care of new concerns that took shape in the Council. As well as these there are the religious congregations, orders, societies, which exist autonomously with their own structures and specific charisms by which they serve the Church. The structure resembles the multidivisional structure of a multinational corporation: there is the central administrative "staff," and there are the functionally oriented "divisions." Since the nineteenth century, the Curia has exercised increasing control over the activities of the universal Church. The result is that the Church has become a highly centralized organization; and because there are no

accountability structures, the bureaucracy can exercise
executive power and control. The Pope is often merely the
figurehead whose signature legitimates control measures
implemented by power alliances behind the scenes.

The exercise of central control is the key element of the
hierarchical clerical model. This model divides the church
neatly into two groups: the "active" clerics who mediate
God's grace, and the "passive" faithful who have no part in
decision making and who achieve salvation by faithfully sub-
mitting to the ministry of the clerics. The whole edifice is
grounded in a dualistic contrast between ordained and laity,
sacred and secular, church and world, spirit and flesh. Given
this understanding, it is not surprising that the "Church" is
identified with "the hierarchy." "The Church thinks," "the
Church teaches," "the Church believes," are expressions
that refer not to what the faithful think or believe, but to the
official position of the hierarchy. As in any hierarchical
structure, power can also be delegated downward when the
functioning of the system so demands by making nonclerics
share in some of the clerical responsibilities (as in the case
of catechists who teach under the supervision of the clerics).
The different services that the faithful (religious and lay)
offer to each other and to the world at large are not seen as
exercising forms of ministry in freedom, but as acts of obedience in carrying out the prescriptions of the Christian way
of life under the control of the clerical class.

When one looks at the New Testament and discovers
the clear affirmation of the gift of the Spirit to all believers
and the call to all to collaborate with the upbuilding of the
church, it appears extraordinary that the task of building
the church became the exclusive duty of a small class of
"ordained ministers." However, the historical reason for
this lay in the inability of the early church to deal with the
conflicting claims to "charism" and "revelation." It is true
that the Montanist and Gnostic heresies nearly destroyed
the early church. But it is also clear that the church panicked

and overreacted by introducing increasingly tighter controls on the claims of spiritual gifts, and restricting them to a governing class with a total monopoly and control of the gifts of the Spirit. In the same way, revelation was declared closed with the death of the last apostle, and the governing class became solely responsible for the faithful keeping of the deposit of faith. With the passing of time, this governing class patterned itself not on models inspired by the gospel but rather on the dominant monarchical model of the surrounding secular society. The church thus became increasingly a power structure obsessed with orthodoxy, uniformity, and control, thereby endangering the gospel values of "diakosis" and "kenosis." But the worst result of all this is that by reducing the faithful to the role of a passive flock the church lost the gifts given to them for the proclamation of the gospel and the upbuilding of the church.

## The Male-Domination of the Church: The Masculine/Feminine Dilemma

We have seen that the culture of economism is male dominated and built exclusively around masculine values. It should not surprise us, therefore, that the pre–Vatican II ecclesial model also demonstrates an exclusive preoccupation with masculine values and attitudes: "unity, continuity, absolute fidelity to tradition, the primacy of authority and the group, the certainty of truth, the God given nature of the church…. The values of this conservative model and its main concerns represent hard (masculine) characteristics" (Esteban 1995:26). All these qualities are unilaterally "left brain" and combine spontaneously to oppress the "feminine." The subjection and denial of "right-brain" feminine values—intuition, cooperation, the value of the God-given person, the centrality of love—have made of the institutional Church a harsh place where the feminine qualities necessary for nurturing life are devalued, and where in consequence the status of women is unequal.

Women constitute a vital and dynamic force within the Church all over the world. They form the majority of the practicing laity and are the nurturers of future Roman Catholic Christians. Yet they are powerless and voiceless within the institutional Church, and are excluded from leadership roles and ordained ministries. Ecclesial structures are patriarchal in all religions, but the male monopoly of ministry in the Roman Catholic Church is grounded in a particularly narrow, traditional understanding of the place of women in the natural order. Thomas Aquinas based his teaching on the Aristotelian view of the patriarchal order of household and state. Because woman is in a state of subjection, he argued, "the female sex cannot signify any superiority of rank" (Summa Theologiae Supp. 39, 1 ad. 1). And because the Church "understands ecclesial authority and power in terms of 'power over,' it has argued that women cannot receive the spiritual power of the sacrament of ordination because of their position of subordination" (Schüssler Fiorenza 1993:295).[9] This essentially naturalist view of the inevitability of woman's status is echoed in the papal encyclical on the dignity and vocation of women (John Paul II 1988). Although the encyclical calls for mutuality of relationship at every level, the assumption here throughout is that the woman "represents a particular value... by the fact of her femininity." It is the attribution of femininity to women and masculinity to men that has legitimated the existence and made possible the power of patriarchy within the Church.

We have already seen that clericalism denies equal functional status to nonordained members of the Church. The effect of patriarchy is similar in that it denies equal status to half its membership, lay and religious. Liturgical symbols, ritual behaviors, and speech about God support a patriarchal and androcentric understanding of the mediation of God's saving power (Collins 1987).[10] Patriarchy is profoundly at odds with the meanings and values of the Kingdom preached by Jesus: "The Jewish *basileia* vision of the gospels, which constitutes the mission and reason for any ecclesial existence, cannot be adequately proclaimed and realized in a patriarchal church. Rather, such a vision can be actualized and affirmed only in a space where women attain full spiritual autonomy, power, self-determination and liberation" (Schüssler Fiorenza 1993:12).

## Conclusion

It may now be clear what we mean by affirming that the church was acculturated to the culture of economism in a way that compromised its capacity to call it to conversion. Both the church and economism play similar power games. (Fig. 2) They carry out their missions from positions of power—a power given by wealth and cultural superiority that is translated into economic and cultural imperialism, and exercised by an authoritarian male class. This power is based on the conviction of the right to conquer the world as a duty to civilize or to convert. This conquest produces a violent transformation and disintegration of the societies affected, and can be sustained only by wielding considerable structural force. The church learned early on to leave the use of force to the secular powers. The power alliance between church and socioeconomic interests may have been uneasy at times and may not always have been intentional, but it has always been seen by the peoples at the receiving end as the two complementary sides of the expansionism of the Christian West. The collaboration of cross and sword is not a myth created by the detractors of Christianity, but a sad historical fact.

The church, because of its own love affair with power, failed to detect the diabolic and idolatrous side of the culture of economism. In the next chapter we explore the way in which people in the church came to realize how, in order to evangelize the dominant culture of economism, the church had to undergo a profound conversion so as to recover the right to speak in God's name to a culture that no longer hears the cries of the poor.

Fig. 2

## CLERICALISM

| VALUE EXCESSES (CONSEQUENCES) | DIFFERENTIATING VALUES | 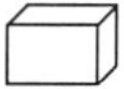 | INTEGRATIVE VALUES | VALUE EXCESSES (CAUSES) |
|---|---|---|---|---|
| destruction of alternative religious systems **leading to** violent resistance to mission | **local** | S Y | **global** | control, centralisation mission as implantation complicity with colonialism |
| destruction of cultural diversity **leading to** acculturation schism | **diversity** | N E | **unity** | universalism, uniformity |
| exclusion from decision-taking processes **leading to** radical dissent | **freedom** | R G | **authority** | authoritarianism, clericalism |
| marginalization of women, **leading to** radical feminism | **feminine** | Y | **masculine** | patriarchy male domination |
| **OPPRESSED   POWERLESS** | **DISINTEGRATION** POWERLESS | | **STRUCTURAL VIOLENCE** POWERFUL | **OPPRESSORS** POWERFUL |

# 4

# The Second Vatican Council: From Power Games to Powerlessness

The Second Vatican Council (1962–65) happened because of a widespread recognition of the need to purify the church from the diabolic within, and was initiated by the vision and foresight of one man. Pope John XXIII opened the floodgates of the Church's "aggiornamento" by convening an ecumenical council—apparently without consultation. The documents for the Council were prepared by the Curia, the bishops were called to assemble in Rome, and the rest, as they say, is history. What in fact happened was that the carefully prepared documents were thrown out by the bishops, the real concerns of the participants surfaced, and the Council that was expected to take three months lasted three years. The Council represented a profound paradigm shift[1] in the Roman Catholic Church: it radically challenged the Church's self-understanding and initiated an ongoing process of searching and reflection that continues to spread ripples throughout the life of the Church. There has been in consequence an enormous culture change, but the paradigm shift is far from complete, because some powerful groups and core hierarchical structures have resisted change and the Church has in consequence become deeply and painfully polarized.[2]

The pressure for change that resulted in the calling of the Council had been building up in the Roman Catholic Church for some time. There were a number of reasons for this. The growth in historical awareness had exposed the church's exclusivism for what it really was—a fundamental departure from gospel insights. In mission territories, the reality of mission had moved from being a crude exercise in church implantation to representing a much more balanced dynamic of gradual adaptation to local circumstances, involving the progressive recognition of values in other cultures and religions. Catholic theology, influenced by the acceptance of historical and biblical criticism, had begun to challenge the self-understanding of the church in a variety of ways.[3] On the pastoral level, movements encouraging the active commitment of lay people in church life gave the lie to the theory of a passive laity, while an atmosphere of openness and tolerance was breaking down the barriers of exclusivity that separated the Roman Catholic Church from other churches and communities.

All of that came to fruition in Vatican II. Seen from one perspective, that historical event was God's call to conversion for the Church. On another level, it was a gigantic effort to contextualize the Church—to bring it out of its self-sufficient ghetto and into the wider context of the modern world. In terms of its own cultural dynamic, the Council shifted the emphasis from a one-sided defense of a set of conservative values to the acceptance of the need to manage the complex value dilemmas faced by the Church in the modern world. This did not involve abandoning any of the traditional values of the Church, but it did involve renouncing the excesses that had crept in because of the one-sidedness of the Church's position. In order to neutralize those excesses, Vatican II began to rediscover a complementary set of values long ignored and neglected, to balance the Church's "masculine values" with another parallel set of "feminine values." There was talk of change and becoming, of the challenge of the future, of freedom, spontaneity, and creativity, of the uniqueness of the human person and the value of diversity, of feeling and subjectivity, of collaboration in community. And above all and in all there was the exploding reality of a God who was not a God of the Church but a God of history, not a God of doctrine but a God of experience, a God who reveals himself in Christ everywhere and in everyone.

It is impossible to convey in a brief chapter the depth and the power of the Council's work. In the new vision, the Church becomes "means" rather than "aim"; it becomes the sign and the means of the transformation of the world into the Kingdom of God, a Kingdom of justice, peace, and love. Behind it all lay the reality of a basic conversion from "power" to "service"[4] of God, of each other, and of the world. New ways of "seeing" and talking (theology/theory) emerged, and with these came new possibilities of being and doing church (pastoral action/praxis). We can summarize the main thrust of the Council's work by identifying the shifts toward balance in each of the Church's key dilemmas.

*The immanence/transcendence dilemma:*
- From a "religion of salvation" to a "religion of structure"; that is, a religion relevant to the structures of daily life;
- From salvation seen as otherworldly to salvation as demanding continuous historical transformation;
- From faith as a "deposit" to faith as continual revelation.

*The continuity/change dilemma:*
- An emphasis on "reading the signs of the times"; on contextualizing the church.

*The unity/diversity dilemma:*
- From an exclusive chosen people to a "sign" of universal salvation;
- From a God of the church to a God of history;
- From conquest to partnership and encounter.

*The authority/freedom dilemma:*
- From clerical control to lay participation;
- From monarchical control to collegiality;
- From delegation to subsidiarity;
- From a "descending" church to an "ascending" church;
- From a teaching church to a learning church;
- From hierarchy to community;
- From "object" to "subject" of evangelization;
- From authoritarianism to collaboration;
- From control to co-responsibility;
- From hierarchical behavior to responsibility hierarchies.

Many would argue that to attempt to schematize the Council's work in this way oversimplifies the issues, because the Council left a great deal of unfinished business, and many of its documents and declarations failed to unravel all the consequences of the insights that struggled to the surface during the time it met. In fact, many of the documents are no more than compromises between the old and the new, and demonstrate the lack of integration of conflicting viewpoints, so that it is not surprising that they lend themselves to divergent interpretations. The fact is that the Council was no more than a beginning of the struggle to rethink the church and its relation to the world at large, and we are left with the difficult task of distinguishing the intention of the Council from the negative historical constraints that obscured that intention.

## The Reception of the Council: Contextual Theologies

The work of the Council generated a new and critical approach in the Roman Catholic Church. It encouraged people to turn outward and to interface with the world, its struggles, and its sufferings. The change of perspective brought a new sensitivity to global suffering and an awareness of the failure of the church to tackle the problems of the oppressed and the causes of oppression. And because the Church's geographical center of gravity had shifted from the prosperous West to the Third World, many people became increasingly aware of the injustice of the world order and of the extent of the Church's responsibility for that injustice. Adherence to a "religion of structure" as opposed to a "religion of salvation" meant that people were no longer content to address the consequences of oppression and injustice by committing their energies to works of mercy; they began to see a need to transform the structures that cause that suffering. Because the Church itself constituted just such a structure, different groups around the world quickly became committed to transforming the structures of the local church and its "praxis" in line with the new ecclesial culture.

Different groups in different parts of the world have shared common concerns in differing oppressive situations. To help and direct the articulation of those concerns so that transformation can occur, those groups have struggled to elaborate a body of theory (theology) that is in fact an "ascending" theology, a theology shaped fundamentally by its context. "Contextual" theology is a new kind of theological reflection—one that emphasizes the social and cultural context of the faith experience and reflects on its meaning in the light of the gospel. All contextual theology is grounded in a view of revelation as interpersonal; God communicates himself in the persons and events of daily life. Christianity, therefore, is incarnational, and reality is sacramental (Bevans 1992:8). Its purpose is thus quite different from traditional "essentialist" theologies that seek only understanding. Contextual theologies aim to implement as praxis the insights implicit in the work of Vatican II. In so doing they all contain a challenge to the traditional structures of the Church, but they also contain a challenge of a deeper kind. Because contextual theology is based in experience, it is not objective in the positivist sense of the word. This implies that truth must mean something other than the absolutist ideas of truth that support traditional theologies and hence legitimate the authority of the hierarchical church.[5]

We believe that it is possible to see contextual theologies as part of an integrated ecclesial response to the suffering caused by the failure of the Church to manage its own organizational cultural dilemmas. The most important areas of contextual theology and praxis in the Roman Catholic Church address precisely those structural fractures that we have identified in analyzing the symbiosis of the hierarchical church paradigm and the culture of economism—socioeconomic oppression, cultural degradation, authoritarianism, and male domination.[6] There is no doubt that the Latin Americans are right to indict the oppressive character of their political and economic structures as the most diabolic aspect of their situation. Those—mainly in Africa and Asia—who see the need for inculturation experience the superimposition of foreign cultures, at both the social and the religious level, as that which oppresses them most. Everywhere in the church there is a growing sympathy with the hurt and frustration of so many people who are deprived of the possibility of using their talents at the service of the church they love by people who cling to their monopoly of ministry. The plight of women everywhere witnesses to their need for justice; this is even more the case in oppressed situations where they find themselves doubly oppressed, as poor and as women.

All contextual theologies share a radical option for the liberation from the destructive consequences of the exploitation of power—political, socioeconomic, or religious—and from the violence that exploitation entails.

- Liberation theology faces up to the consequences of socioeconomic oppression (Gutierrez 1973; Boff 1985; Segundo 1974).

- The theology of inculturation addresses the pain of cultural disintegration (Shorter 1988; Panikkar 1981; Arbuckle 1990).

- The theology of collaborative ministry seeks to redress the waste of gifts and talents inherent in the practice of authoritarian clericalism (Provost 1984; Bausch 1988; Sofield and Juliano 1987).

- Feminist theology questions the discrimination of women and the oppression of the feminine (Fabella and Oduyoye 1988; Chung 1990; Thistlethwaite 1989).

These different but complementary theologies share three common characteristics: an option of solidarity with the oppressed, a collaborative strategy, and the fact of constituting a challenge to the previous dominant hierarchical institutional culture.

1. Although the "preferential option for the poor" is most closely associated with liberation theology, all contextual theologies are characterized by a shift in the basis from which the church is seen to evangelize. A church that is part of the power structures cannot preach the gospel. Mission can be done only by a church prepared to witness in *solidarity with the oppressed,* be they the socioeconomically marginalized, the culturally impoverished, those deprived of participation, or the women oppressed.

2. All contextual theologies demand a shift from authoritarian structures to a collaborative involvement of people in the solution of their own problems. All contextual theologies believe in the integrating and healing (symbolic) character of community as the only way to overcome the diabolic side of oppression. In a *collaborative strategy* a communitarian culture replaces the hierarchical individualism of a dominant culture, which depersonalizes and reduces persons to objects.[7] When people are reduced to consumers they lose their humanity. When people lose

their culture they lose their identity. The lack of participation in organizational decision making allows people to be manipulated. The exploitation of women reduces them to sex objects and beasts of burden. (And let us not forget that in all forms of violent abuse, the abuser is as much depersonalized as the abused, if not more so.)

- Liberation theology sees "basic ecclesial communities," where all are called to theologize, as the means and the result of socioeconomic liberation (Boff 1985:125–30).

- The theology of inculturation asks for the creation of "small Christian communities" as the subject of inculturation (Shorter 1988:211–12).

- The theology of collaborative ministry advocates the cooperation of all "gifted" Christian people by extending ministry to all the baptized and involving all in communal discernment and decision making at all the levels of the church's structures (Cooper 1993).

- Feminist theologians call on the solidarity of all women as the prerequisite for the overcoming of male domination (King 1994).

3. All contextual theologies contain an *institutional challenge.* The implications of what was said and proclaimed in the safe and splendid confines of St. Peter's in Rome become apparent when praxis-oriented theological reflection is taken to its logical consequences. Vatican II represented a call to radical ecclesial conversion. The demand for change was based on the conviction that the church itself had to change in order to become credible as a missionary church; that is, as an instrument for the transformation of the world. But ecclesial change was bound to have much wider sociopolitical consequences, and the contextual theologies reflected this. Thus:

- Liberation theology denounces the marriage of the institutional church with the dominant and exploitative social classes and structures in Latin America and enjoins the church to publicly break that link.

- The theology of inculturation asks the Latin church to abandon its superiority complex, its universalism, and its cultural imperialism to allow the growth of a really multicultural church.

- The theology of collaborative ministry is a frontal challenge to clericalism and demands the participation of laity and religious in decision making at all the levels of the church's structures.

- Feminist theology denounces not only the marginalization of women and the male monopoly of ministry in the church, but the oppressive character of a one-sided masculine church culture.

Although contextual theologies were only giving substance to the organizational cultural shift that started to take shape in the documents of the Vatican Council, it was overoptimistic to think that an institution as complex and large as the Roman Catholic Church, with its deeply traditional roots and feelings, could simply align the structures of all its institutions to the new culture in a short space of time without major trouble. "Taking the side of the oppressed" may be a strategy demanded by the gospel, but it is not surprising that many of those responsible for the operation of church institutions became a little nervous when faced with such a barrage of demands for institutional change. Furthermore, there was a real danger that the pendulum would swing too far in the other direction, and that the excesses of conservatism would be replaced with the excesses of revolution.

### The Reception of the Council: Revolution

After centuries in which the Roman Catholic Church opted for continuity, the Council encouraged it to change. What was needed was the eventual achievement of a balance between continuity and change, but this was not properly understood by either conservatives or progressives. There was a widespread tendency to understand change as requiring a complete rupture with all traditional values and practices. Many in the church swung from the rigidities of conservatism to the excesses of the progressives, from a total resistance to change to the excesses of revolution: anti-institutionalism, militant dissent, anarchic individualism, anti-intellectualism, relativism, activism, and so on.

Change without continuity is not only a one-sided solution; it also leads in the end to anarchy and chaos. Furthermore, in the call to change lurked a dangerous revolutionary temptation that carried with it precisely the same potential for violence as did the authoritarian exercise of power.[8] Every contextual theology has undergone the temptation to go down that road. If the church shaped by a hierarchical model had its ambiguities, so also did the organizations, communities, and movements shaped by the various contextual theologies. It was often possible to discern a sharp revolutionary edge in the movements associated with contextual theologies. Priests took up arms and advocated an armed class struggle in the name of liberation theology. There was an acritical emphasis on "primitivism" and a purging of any outside influence in the name of the theology of inculturation. Radical democracy in the Church was advocated to replace clericalism in the name of collaborative ministry, and feminist theology occasionally ignored the need to collaborate with male colleagues. Unfortunately, those excesses, which often went well beyond the "espoused theories" of the leaders, provided an excuse for the institutions defending the status quo to discard out of hand any demand for change. None of this is surprising in view of the fact that the invitation to change was issued to a Church that was historically conditioned to think in an either/or mind-set. We had not been trained to manage dilemmas; we only knew how to defend values unilaterally and to back up that defense with the use of power. It was difficult to realize that the new culture demanded not that we reject those values and replace them with an alternative set of values, but that we adopt the both/and mind-set needed to keep opposing perspectives in tension.

### The Reception of the Council: Resistance

Paradigm shifts demand a radical and total conversion, and because every conversion is painful, paradigm shifts will usually be opposed by the "establishment." The establishment will marshall its power and its resources in defense of the established paradigm against the "prophets" of the new paradigm, even when the paradigm shift is introduced by an Ecumenical Council, which in theory speaks for the Roman Catholic Church as a whole. This is what in fact happened after the Council. Because it was impossible to get the balance between change and continuity right at the first try, the church became hopelessly polarized between those who advocated change and those who resisted change and clung to the existing hierarchical culture.

The decade after the Council was a time of turmoil. Many in the church found it extremely difficult to make the transition toward a church where unity is lived in diversity, where integration happens in the midst of growing differentiation. Diversity demands a radical lessening of central control. But diversity can be seen as divisive, and there is great temptation to reinforce central control in order to counteract the threat of schism. It is easier to change ideas than attitudes, especially the attitudes implicit in a culture of power. Also, after centuries of control it is very difficult to operate as a culture of trust.

The truth is that nobody was really ready for the radicality of the change initiated by the Council. The life changes demanded by the Council were too much for many, both priests and lay people. Many priests and religious did not feel up to the challenge and left. Many tried to adapt and were discouraged by misunderstandings with those in authority; in the end they also left or became cynical. Many others, at all levels from bishops to lay people, simply refused to budge and continued to act as if the Council had not happened. There is an anecdote about the Archbishop of Dublin coming back from the Council and answering questions at the airport from journalists who asked him what changes would happen as a result of the Council: "In Ireland, very little," was the Archbishop's answer. Even more common was the frequent very simplistic and superficial assimilation of the Council not only on the part of the laity but even among priests and religious. This lack of understanding produced stress because of the tensions and conflicts that the changes created.

It is important to emphasize the seriousness of the polarization in the church, because it imposes enormous constraints on anything that we want to achieve. We may seriously believe that changing and adapting in answer to the needs of the times is today the only way to be faithful to the gospel, but there are many in the Church who feel deeply threatened by any change. We have to recognize that change in any form produces anxiety in people with a very deep-seated need of uncertainty avoidance (Hofstede 1991). Not surprisingly, there have been many who, scared to death, have rushed to shore up the old conservative church edifice in order to safeguard the feeling of security that went with it.

### The Reception of the Council: Restorationism

During the present pontificate, conservatism has hardened into restorationism. Restorationism is "an ill-defined but nonetheless powerful movement within the Church towards the *uncritical* reaffirmation of pre–Vatican II structures and attitudes" (Arbuckle 1993:3). There has been a strong growth of movements that actively espouse the old ecclesial culture in the name of fidelity to traditional values. These groups have gained considerable influence in the corridors of ecclesial power.[9] Their views are above all ideological: their vision is not a return to the gospel but the restoration of a "Christian world order," a theocracy, where there is no place for dialogue, in which the church can dictate public and personal morality, and in which intolerance creates the social pressure that controls the life of the individual.

In the context of mission, restorationism advocates a return to "implantation": the re-evangelization of rapidly de-Christianizing countries is to be achieved by the involvement of the laity in gaining control of the levers of social power in order to influence policy at the service of the defense of "Christian" moral values. There is an acritical identification of the gospel with one particular culture, and evangelization is identified with the rebuilding of that supposedly universally valid culture. This integrative outlook on evangelization, by identifying the church and the gospel with one particular culture, precludes any meaningful discussion of the relationship between gospel and culture in a pluri-cultural church and in a pluri-cultural world. In fact, it sees in pluralism the main evil to be eliminated: there is only one truth; there is only one way (Esteban 1994).

Restorationism totally sidelines not only the rethinking of the Council but also all the concerns and contextual theologies that have sprung up in its wake. Much of the impetus generated by Vatican II is now stalled. The high point of liberation theology has passed, and many of its most outspoken leaders have been silenced. There is much talk about inculturation, but at the same time there is a concerted effort to bring the whole area of mission under direct Vatican control. The great wave of reflection and experiment in collaborative ministry of the seventies has been succeeded by cynicism because of the persistence of authoritarian structures and hierarchical behavior. Feminist theological reflection seems after all to be going nowhere in a Church that categorically refuses to recognize the gifts women can bring to partnership in ministry. What is more, contextual theologies are all denounced by restorationism as dangerous deviations undermining the authority and the cohesion of the church:

- Liberation theology undermines the power that the church needs in order to carry out its God-given mission and endangers the social order by inciting the oppressed to revolution, influenced as it is by an atheistic Marxism analysis and the espousing of the class struggle.

- The theology of inculturation critically endangers the unity of the church by exposing it to the divisiveness of tribalism and nationalism.

- The call to collaborative ministry totally undermines the sacramental power of the ordained ministers and compromises in that way their unique and essential role in the transmission of salvation.

- Feminists simply want to subvert (1) God's created order in which women are subservient to men, and (2) Jesus' clear wish to confine the church exclusively to the care of a male- ordained ministry.

Restorationism is no more than an attack of collective vertigo occasioned by the need to face the radical demands of the paradigm shift of church and mission. Different groups of people in the church cannot imagine how the church can carry out its mission except from a position of power and privilege. But if the governing structures of the church succumb to that vertigo by siding with the restorationists, the current painful polarization in the church could become a permanent structural split. In fact, the current situation in the Roman Catholic Church is a real example of what we earlier termed "schismogenesis, a growing split in the structure of ideas" (Hampden-Turner 1994:19). In this kind of situation, "it is... common for leaders to prevent their own disintegration by siding with one clique or faction against the others. In this way they 'save' themselves, yet the organization is severed" (19–20). This risk exists at the moment in the Church, where the central governing structures seem to be siding more and more with the restorationists by clinging ferociously to the pre-Council organizational culture. A victory for the restorationists would surely save the church as an organization, but it would "fatally cripple the organization's capacity to learn" (20) and result in the loss for the Church of many of its most forward-looking and creative movements, groups, and leaders. It would also render the Church incapable of recovering its commitment to preach the Good News of the Kingdom to the culture of economism.

### *Metanoia*: from Power to Service

The foregoing account of the aftermath of the Second Vatican Council demonstrates that the one factor that lies at the root of all the problems in the Church is the attachment to power. The reality of power is the root cause of the oppressive consequences of the symbiosis between the culture of economism and the Church: it is the love of power that has prevented the Church from distancing itself from that culture so as to be able to challenge it. Contextual theologies, because they echo the cries of the poor, identify and challenge the "taskmasters" at the root of oppression. However, they fail to address the real issues to the degree that they advocate a transfer of power from the oppressors to the oppressed. Revolutions do not solve the problems because they perpetuate the use of power.

The radical self-criticism represented by the work of Vatican II set the Church on the long road back to self-discovery. That same journey removed the Church some distance away from the values and the mind-set of the dominant Western culture. But the radicality and the aggressiveness of the new ecclesiologies triggered a counterrevolution that resulted in deep divisions within the Church. The resultant polarization needs to be resolved, and it cannot be resolved by a refusal to change. But it can be resolved by demonstrating to those who do refuse to change that there is a way forward that safeguards their most cherished concerns. What we have to show is that the only way to save all the traditional values while purifying them from their diabolic excesses is by a conversion that renounces power.

The *metanoia* ("change of heart") represented by the abandonment of power would be the Church's answer to God's call to conversion. It would facilitate a trusting collaboration between conservatives who feel the attraction of the old value system and progressives who feel the need for change and the attraction of the new organizational culture hinted at by the Council. It would enable the achievement of a creative tension between all the opposing value dilemmas with which we are faced, of continuity and change, of the memory of the past and the dream of the future, of authority and freedom, of unity and diversity, of reason and feeling, of the masculine and the feminine, of the divine and the human. (Fig. 3) It would bring about a symbolic encounter where the violence needed to keep change at bay is replaced by a synergy in which opposing values enhance each other.

What the Roman Catholic Church needs is a conversion from an authoritarian hierarchical organization to a communitarian, participative one. Such a conversion is the prerequisite for mission to the culture of economism, because it is only in the conversion experience of the encounter of its opposing values that the Church can recover its integrity and its commitment to preach the Kingdom. It is only by the exercise of trusting the different, the "other" within the Church, that the Church can learn to trust the "other" in cultural terms. It is only by being seen to renounce its attachment to power that it can be credible to a culture wearied by the violence of power. It is only by distancing itself from the structures of power that the Church can condemn the taskmasters and become a liberator. All this is reminiscent of another story, told a long time ago, about someone who was asked to take his shoes off before being sent as liberator to free a people from captivity. He was sent in powerlessness so that all could see that it was in the power and in the name of the One who sent him that the people were freed (Exod. 3:1–15). And, much later, there was another man who liberated the whole of humanity by the powerlessness of his death on a cross. This man called his death an act of service. Perhaps it is only by replacing power with service that the world can be liberated from oppression. And if that is the case, the Church must not only renounce power, it must take off its shoes and opt to serve the world. It is this notion of service that must underpin the mission to economism.

Fig. 3

## CONSEQUENCES OF VATICAN II— FROM POWER-GAMES TO POWERLESSNESS

| EXCESSES | VALUES | SYNERGY | VALUES | EXCESSES |
|---|---|---|---|---|
| revolution, rupture, anti-ritualism | CHANGE (becoming) | adaptating (inculturation), reading the signs of the times | CONTINUITY (being) | traditionalism, restorationism, rubricism |
| schism | DIVERSITY (particular, differentiating) | communion, unity in diversity | UNITY (universal, integrating) | universalism, uniformity |
| anarchy, chaos, radical dissent | FREEDOM (enabling, autonomy, decentralisation, dissent) | collaborating with a 'responsibility hierarchy', (collegiality, subsidiarity) | AUTHORITY (constraining, heteronomy, centralisation, loyalty) | authoritarianism, clericalism, legalism, control |
| anti-intellectualism, relativism | FEELING | faith as process, inclusivism | REASON | dogmatism, absolutism |
| PROGRESSIVE | | nurturing, community, service, powerlessness | CONSERVATIVE | |

# 5

# Christian Mission to the Culture of Economism

Vatican II called the Church to renew its commitment to the gospel, and in part the Church has responded to that call. It is in that response that we see the possibilities for mission to the culture of economism. Mission is the task of bringing the Good News, of calling people to repent because the Kingdom of God is near at hand. But differing views exist not only as to how that task should be carried out, but also as to the ways in which missionary activity should be interpreted. In recent decades there have been major changes in the understanding of mission in the Roman Catholic Church, and there currently are competing and coexisting viewpoints. (Fig. 4) In the model of *mission as implantation,* the most exclusivistic position, the "good news" is brought to "pagans" who then become "passive recipients of the Christian message and passive consumers of European 'Christian' culture" (Shorter 1994:69). In return, these pagans convert by abandoning their religion and becoming members of the Roman Catholic Church. The "means of salvation" are made available through the implantation of Church structures.

After the Second World War the work of a number of theologians (mainly French speaking) advocated the recognition of the values in the cultures to which mission was

Fig. 4

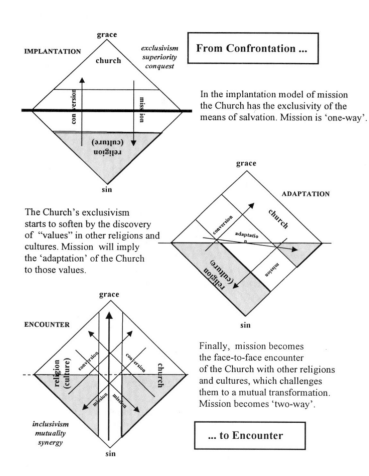

**From Confrontation ...**

In the implantation model of mission the Church has the exclusivity of the means of salvation. Mission is 'one-way'.

The Church's exclusivism starts to soften by the discovery of "values" in other religions and cultures. Mission will imply the 'adaptation' of the Church to those values.

Finally, mission becomes the face-to-face encounter of the Church with other religions and cultures, which challenges them to a mutual transformation. Mission becomes 'two-way'.

**... to Encounter**

addressed. They proposed a new understanding of *mission as adaptation* that still enjoins conversion to Christianity because it is the only true religion, but at the same time tries to respect the values of others. This is done by an adaptation of missionary structures and methods to these values as they are discovered. This is the model that was accepted in Vatican II,[1] and it is today the most widespread operative model of mission for missionaries in the field. It is still an asymmetrical understanding of mission, but its faults are moderated by the mutual enrichment that mission brings to all concerned.

Vatican II did not put an end to the development of new understandings of mission. During the time of the Council, German and Dutch theologians were already developing a "theology of non-Christian religions" that recognized not only the existence of values in other religions but the salvific value of religions as such. This inclusive theology of mission considers *mission as encounter* between the gospel and the cultures encountered in the context of mission. All those concerned in that salvific encounter are called to conversion in the search for new instances of synthesis between the gospel and other religious cultures. It is this process that has come later to be called inculturation. Through this encounter others are invited to share in the Christian faith experience in such a way that their religious and cultural past is reformed around that experience. At the same time, this encounter challenges the cultural presuppositions of the missionaries themselves. The model of conversion implied by this understanding of mission therefore implies both a symmetry and a mutuality. This perspective constitutes a radical challenge to the exclusivism of previous models, but we have still a long way to go before it becomes the mainstream missionary approach in the Roman Catholic Church. However, we believe that it is the understanding of mission as encounter that will yield the most valuable insights into the challenges faced by mission to economism.

The basis for the development of this view of "mission as encounter" is rooted in the work of the Second Vatican Council. The recognition by the Council of God's transforming presence outside the visible frontiers of the Church represented a major shift in thinking. So also did the shift in philosophical presuppositions. The epistemological basis of all the Council's work was the "turn to the subject," the grounding of all knowledge in experience as opposed to "objective" or empirical reality.[2] In the documents of the Council there were clear examples of the way in which experience was used to generate reflection and inspire new and creative insights.[3] But it is in the case of mission in particular that the grounding of thought in experience has triggered deep and continual reassessment, particularly by missionaries themselves, of the meaning of their own experience and the light it sheds on the nature of mission.[4]

## Mission as Encounter

Mission as encounter is best illustrated by a story. Like all good stories, this is the story of an experience. It has taken one of us twenty years since coming back from Africa to make some sense of what happened to him and many others like him there. It has taken all that time to work through the overlay of theological and cultural presuppositions in order to describe accurately what happened in an experience of eight years in the north of Ghana, and the rethinking is ongoing. (It is worthwhile to mention that the concrete experience had the best of possible preparations—doctoral work on the validity of the salvific value of non-Christian religions.)

In this experience, a missionary priest, belonging to a missionary society and representing a human institution— the Roman Catholic Church—developed over a length of time a number of relationships of varying depths with a number of people, very few of them Christian, belonging to the Dagomba ethnic group. The friendship and solidarity of that priest with the people, motivated by a desire to bring the

Christian gospel and the love of God to them, brought not only some relief in time of suffering and need, but also joy and peace on many occasions of formal and informal contact—most memorable of all, the privilege of having been allowed to walk with some of them on their last steps in this life. God knows that there was enough wrong with them to denounce and to reform. But all that could never overshadow what the Dagomba shared with him: a language as a way to their universe and to their hearts; unlimited hospitality; endless entertainment; a sharing in their myths and cherished common memories; their sense of humor in adversity; their ability to celebrate life; their sense of ritual as cosmic reconciliation; a participation in their joys, their sorrows, their quarrels, and their dreams; a taste of their food; a sense of their dignity and unbounded admiration for their proud horsemanship; the heartbeat of their drums with its gift of *ecstasis*, in celebration and its soothing power for sleep. That whole wealth of human wisdom and richness of experience forms today the basis of a course on African religions for students from all over the world, including Africa.

And in the midst of all that came the greatest gift of all, to be made aware, through exchanges in which some of those Africans shared their deepest hurts and feelings, of precisely those diabolic shadows that we are trying to exorcise here— the threat to their world from "our" white man's economic and cultural imperialism, paternalism, and racism. This was cogent plea for radical conversion if ever there was one!

At the end of a few years, there was little trace of superiority and clearly no reason for it, no basis in fact for exclusivity, and surely no desire to conquer. The missionary had been graced by the amazing discovery that there were other ways of being human, ways that overflowed with life-loving and a life-giving energy. It was clear that God had been waiting for him, there in the middle of Africa, completely unexpectedly. The missionary found that it was he who had to repent, because the Kingdom of God was really at hand, there, among the Dagombas.

That experience challenges all the fundamental presuppositions of previous models of mission, every notion of religious, human, or cultural superiority, and every notion of exclusivity. In particular, it confirms the validity of the search for a new paradigm of "church" by the Second Vatican Council, because it invalidates the idea of a perfect "teaching" church. What we discover in the missionary encounter is first of all that the church is far from perfect and—much more important—that it has everything to learn from and about the peoples whom it intends to evangelize. The missionary experience shows that God is more mysterious than we thought and does not play by our rules. We were not ready for that. It is vital that we learn to listen, because God is waiting for us elsewhere to call us to radical "conversion."

Missionaries are generally not ready even today to take that kind of experience at face value, to be themselves evangelized in the process of meeting people of other faiths and cultures. Although there is an ongoing process of self-discovery, there are still many people in the church who wear cultural blinkers, or who are too busy simply surviving to take time to make sense of what is happening to them. But there are also others who attempt to make sense of the experience, common to many missionaries of being evangelized in the process of evangelizing. What we are discovering is that in that experience there is both a template for the understanding of interpersonal encounters and the basis of a renewed theological model of mission that can revolutionize the way the church relates to others.[5] But adjusting the model of mission from pure implantation to adaptation does not go far enough; we really need to start from scratch if we are to develop a theological understanding that privileges the authenticity of experience.

There is one simple reason why the story told above requires us to rethink our whole understanding of mission. All previous models of mission are fundamentally "one way." God sends the church to bring the gospel to the four corners of the earth; mission calls people to conversion, and that conversion in its full historical form leads to baptism. But that is only one side of the reciprocal dynamic affecting all the realities in the encounter. God sends not only the church to others; God sends others to the church. We were fooled by the fact of the physical displacement of the missionaries into thinking that was of the essence of mission. The essence of mission is not the displacement but the encounter at the end of it. And it takes at least two to have an encounter. In that encounter there is a mutuality, a reciprocity, a symmetry. In fact, there is a two-way evangelization. Mission was supposed to teach the Africans how to be Christian. But experience seems to point to something deeper. In the process of mutual encounter, whereby the missionary and the African become open to each other, receptive to the difference of the "other," mission encourages the Africans to become authentically African and in the process teaches the church how to become really Christian. It is only the willingness to convert as a consequence of encounter with others that gives the missionary the right to challenge those others to the same process of conversion. That challenge is implicit in the encounter and is there long before it is expressed in words.

One day an old Dagomba man, a friend, came to see the missionary. After the customary long greetings, the old man asked whether his grandchildren could be accepted into the Roman Catholic school so that they could become Christians. The reason he gave for this request has lived in the heart of the missionary ever since. "You, the Fara,[6] are very strange people. You are rich and care for the poor. You are white and love the blacks. You are foreigners and speak our language. You are young and have the wisdom of the old. But, most important of all, you have something we do not have. You have mercy. I am too old to change and become like you. But I would like my grandchildren to become Christian so that they too can have mercy."

This story illustrates the way in which the process of encounter reveals the capacity of the Christian faith to liberate what is genuinely African, or Asian, or Latin American. The church converts the Africans by challenging them to abandon their diabolic side, and the Africans in the same process convert the church by challenging it to be genuinely Christian—not an agent of oppression, but a community in solidarity with the poor, respectful of the variety of cultures. It frees the creativity of all its members, gives women real equality with men and frees the feminine, and strives to establish in all a nonexploitative relationship with the earth. Such a church is genuinely at the service of those it is sent to and abandons power for the sake of reconciliation and synergy.

## A Theology of Mission as Encounter

Encounter is more than just a model for the understanding of mission; it is the event that lies at the heart of human existence (Buber 1937), and to understand mission as encounter is therefore to situate its reality in the profound context of being and identity. For Martin Buber, "all real living is meeting" (Ketcham 1978:27), because it is in the encounter with people, with things, and with God that our "I," our identity, is established. "We can understand ourselves by starting from the other or from others, and only by starting from them" (Marcel 1951:8). Each encounter is unique; some encounters are more meaningful than others. We encounter others who share our cultural conditioning in comfortable, nonchallenging, superficial Me-You relationships that serve merely to reinforce our cultural identity. We encounter the world around us in I-It relationships that tell us "what" we are. Neither of these encounters touches the depths of our being. It is only in the I-Thou encounter that we become "who" we are, because that encounter creates and reveals new aspects of our being. It finds us and alters us so that we are not the same again because it is self-revelatory. Such encounter "comes, and it comes to bring *you* out; if it does not reach you, meet you, then it vanishes; but it comes back in another form. It is not outside of you, it stirs in the depth of you; if you say 'Soul of my soul' you have not said too much" (Buber 1937:32–33).

The contingency of my own being, my own identity, on relation with others is paralleled by the contingency of my being on the Being by whom I am addressed, the God whom I encounter in all other encounters. In the Christ-event the Being of God is made publicly and personally accessible in a new way, so that the "other" person or group of persons whom I meet in any human situation is the concrete manifestation of the "Kingdom near at hand."

God is the OTHER, transcendent;
    but the God whom nobody has seen comes to ME in others
    in order that I may become "other," God-like.
It is by recognizing the OTHER in the others (strangers)
    that we may overcome "otherness" in TOGETHERNESS
    (symbolism).
In encounter, WE are challenged to transcend ourselves
    so as to become the OTHER for others (mission),
    to do away with all "otherness" (diabolic)
    in a radical TOGETHERNESS that respects the "other"
    by a surrender (service) to the other as OTHER.
Our TOGETHERNESS (the symbolic) is God the OTHER
    becoming US (Emmanuel—God with us—immanent).
In TOGETHERNESS the world is reconciled.

In the missionary encounter God draws the church, which habitually accommodates to the surrounding cultures and is therefore deeply ambiguous,[7] into an encounter with other religions/cultures that are also ambiguous and blind to their own diabolic side, so that in coming together both may be converted. As with all encounters, that encounter is a concrete encounter in time and space between people: in the confrontation there is a conversion, a change of orientation toward the world on both sides, because the encounter changes the people. The "church" is challenged to convert because, by exposing itself to the Spirit that works in the other religion/culture, it becomes aware of its own diabolic side. The "culture/religion" is challenged to conversion because its shadows are progressively illumined by the Spirit that works in the church. That mutual conversion may lead to their coming progressively together in one single community of faith, or it may result in struggling for mutual conversion in an autonomous existence. In any case, through the encounter and from the first moment of it, the risks of ambiguity are willingly accepted, and the Kingdom of God is brought nearer.

### The Encounter with Economism:
### a Two-Way Evangelization

This theology of encounter, tentative as it is, suggests the outlines of a salvific relationship between the church and the culture of economism. In earlier chapters we argued that such a relationship was not possible because of the symbiotic links between church and culture. For centuries the Christian church and Western culture have lived in a comfortable, acculturated side-by-side "Me-You" relationship. But many things have now changed. The reforms began by the Second Vatican Council have moved the Roman Catholic Church from its rigidly universalist and exclusivist position, and allowed it to become aware that the Spirit works in all places and in all cultures, including the Western secular culture of economism. Within the secular culture there has also been a shift in perspective, particularly within organizations. The awareness of the basic failure of economism and its institutions to produce human happiness and of its power to demolish so much that is good in the world has left many people confused and depressed. People who have wholeheartedly espoused the causes of economism and who have given all their energies to the management of its organizations now feel an urgent need to reassess their values in the light of their responsibility for steering their organizations into an uncertain future. Having trusted the beneficial hand of the market for so long, they now seek new ways of incorporating a value perspective into business decisions. It is not only people in the church who have been looking for new ways of being "church"; people in organizations have also been searching for new ways of being "organization."[8]

It would appear, then, that the institutional church and the institutions of the culture of economism are ready to encounter each other as ontologically and culturally different realities. In that encounter each will meet the challenge to convert, to become "other," to abandon the diabolic and seek the symbolic by recognizing in the "other" the key to each's authenticity and integrity. The conversion required is an institutional one in both cases. Stories of encounter speak of persons, but when the missionary encountered the Dagombas he brought Christ in his church to the encounter, and the Dagombas brought their Spirit-filled culture. Although the encounter between church and economism must always be an encounter between persons, these persons bring to the situation that aspect of their being and of their existence that needs to experience that encounter. The encounter is then between people as part of the institutional church on the one hand, and people who work in and with the organizations of the culture of economism on the other, and as such is an encounter between two cultures. In this "I-Thou" encounter, each culture will challenge the other to conversion, because in the identity of each is something that speaks to a need for conversion in the other.

## Aspects of Encounter

If we reflect on the story of the missionary and the Dagombas, we can identify the aspects of that encounter that can help us to understand something of the nature of "mission to economism." The essence of mission is that it is a two-way challenge to conversion. The encounter of church and economism will call forth a response to the need of the other; it will require an openness, a willingness to share, and a receptivity to what is shared; it will entail a recognition of the value of the encounter in terms of the gift of identity, and a recovery of wholeness and purpose. The perspective is not one of implantation, but rather one of incarnation.

### Response to Need

The church is composed of those whose identities have been effected and affected through their encounter with God in the Christ-event (Ketcham 1978:153); it is a community that shares that common identity. But the influence of the past and the divisiveness of power make that identity less visible to others, and in the Roman Catholic Church the "I-It" nature of hierarchy threatens the "I-Thou" of ecclesial community. The Church is in need of conversion; it needs to learn how to recover its missionary identity and to realize it in an organizational culture that is appropriate for that task. It cannot do this by looking into the church tradition or the biblical message. Vatican II did propose a new organizational culture for the church, but the Church has had to admit that it does not know how to be the Church the Council hinted at. It is one thing to encourage the Church to abandon a centuries-old hierarchical organizational paradigm and to propose the main theoretical outlines of a new organizational culture based on the idea of community, but it is quite another to translate that vision into working blueprints for all the levels of the Church's structure. The people who know about organizations and organizational change are in the world of business and corporations and involved in related academic research. In order to become an organizational culture that, at all its complex levels, learns to manage its dilemmas in a way that avoids the excesses of the past, the Church might benefit by enlisting the help of those in business and organizational theory and practice who are dealing precisely with those dilemmas.

Organizations are being called upon to respond to the conflicting challenges they face on every side. These pressures are not only the more immediate result of global competitive and technological developments; they are also the wider consequences of the "critical juncture" in which we are "caught between the remnants of an industrial society with its paradoxes of progress and exploitation, and the promise of a post modern society with its emphasis on sustainability and transformation" (Bilmoria et al 1994:71). In the face of these pressures, organizations have discovered their need to identify and articulate their values (Ghoshal and Bartlett 1994, 1995a, 1995b), to move from the excesses of one-sided "masculine" values: from conflict to cooperation, from domination to partnership, from individualism to community, from exploitation to stewardship, from alienation to nurturing. "Organizations are searching for their deepest values, corporations are struggling with how to be socially responsible, work is being shaped by quality-of-life considerations, and new definitions of success are being proposed to replace traditional standards and criteria" (Bilmoria et al 1994:74). The most significant element in this search for meaning and value is the growing awareness that the global context of organizational activity and the role of large companies in creating the "global village" have profound implications not only for business but for the future of humanity itself. The church has a long history of global involvement; it exists as a living force in most places around the world; and it has the kind of centralized experience and resources that might assist international business to articulate and implement the values that it seeks to adopt in the context of global business.

### Receptivity to What Is Shared;
### Openness and Willingness to Disclose

Both the Roman Catholic Church and the organizations of economism are, for different reasons, facing unprecedented pressures to change. They can no longer remain in the comfortable backwaters of tradition; they can no longer rely on custom and practice to ensure an adequate response to challenges. What is called for is no less than organizational transformation. The Church finds itself in the uncomfortable position of having to become a learning organization after many centuries of thinking of itself as a teaching one. We have discovered after the Council how difficult it is to reorganize, how slow and frustrating it can be. Different organizations in the Church—particularly religious societies that enjoy a certain degree of autonomy—have been trying to find constructive compromises between the authoritarianism of the old model on the one hand and revolution on the other. Efforts have also been made at "ground level" that have resulted in the growth of Christian communities inspired by the contextual theologies. However, the main problem has been that the basic structural backbone of the Church—the hierarchical clerical structure with its central administration—has not fundamentally changed.

But business organizations have long experience of structural change and adaptation. In particular, they have a wealth of theoretical knowledge and practical experience concerning the failure of the hierarchical model in complex organizations. "Bounded rationality" leads to inefficient and inappropriate decision making; authoritarianism stifles the creativity and initiative that is surely a manifestation of the Spirit at work; and lack of consultative processes removes the possibility of harnessing talents and creating the synergic know-how that is the essential groundwork of mission, Christian or secular. The Church needs to hear the stories of the world of organizations—stories of failure, of confusion, of organizational "death"—so it has the chance to develop an understanding that enables it to see its own situation through the eyes of others.

Secular organizations learned a long time ago that culture formation and culture change in learning organizations are interwoven with patterns and styles of leadership. Leadership style has to do with the way leaders at every level in the organization enable and empower others. Seen from that perspective, the main obstacle to the acceptance of a new organizational culture within the Church resides in a kind of transactional leadership that is set in continuity and does not know how to become a transformational leadership capable of steering change. It is this change in leadership style that is the fundamental change demanded in the church today. Transformational leaders are vision-creators, designers, stewards, listeners. They are teachers in the sense that they are coaches who help people to develop a perspective on the whole organizational system that will enable them to play their part in the future. They help to bring the organization from where it is to where it wants to be by facilitating the process of organizational learning in this way. But above all, transformational leaders are servants; the most effective leaders are those who aspire to serve first in order to lead, rather than those who aspire to lead first (Senge 1994). The Church could do well to share in the insights of organizational reflection on leadership in the light of its own understanding of biblical views on servant leadership. In particular, it needs to hear about ways to facilitate organizational learning so that people can be trained for lay mission.

Organizations too experience obstacles to the kind of change they know is necessary. The old strategy-structure-systems definition of corporate architecture relied for its effectiveness on a standardization of human behavior that threatened loyalty and motivation (Ghoshal and Bartlett 1994). But in a climate of change, of restructuring, de-layering, and downsizing, employee commitment is essential if the organization is to survive. Companies have to adopt new philosophies, move to new paradigms that make sense not only to those who work for the organization but also to the wider stakeholder constituency. Objectives have to be redefined in terms of purpose as opposed to strategy; targets have to be set in terms of achievable states of affairs rather than in terms of bland financial statistics. Such redefinition will require companies to decide on what they believe in, what they stand for—in other words, to articulate organizational values in a way that will attract and retain the loyalty of employees and satisfy the needs of managers for meaning and job satisfaction. Beliefs, values, and purpose demand a source, an origin. The Church can contribute to the ongoing search process for this source.

### Recognition of Mutual Challenge to Conversion

An encounter between the Roman Catholic Church and the culture of economism will ultimately lead to a recognition of the nature of the mutual challenge that each poses to the other. The challenge is nothing less than a challenge to abandon the diabolic and seek the symbolic by recognizing in the other the key to its own authenticity. The outcome, the ultimate prize, will be an integration of the respective strengths of both while at the same time fostering the elimination of respective weaknesses. There is a real sense in which it is possible to envisage the direction that this process might take. The reality of the Church is that it is above all a community of faith: it exists to witness to the reality of the Kingdom in every sphere of human existence, and by witnessing to realize its identity as a Church that calls all men and women to Christ. Its organizational dimension exists only to facilitate that mission. But to the extent that the Church loses that apostolic self-understanding, sees its own reality in terms of tradition and hierarchy rather than in terms of a faith community, it fails to give a credible witness to a secular world that is fully aware of the necessity for unity of purpose and practice. In spite of the fact that Vatican II recalled the Church to its identity as a community, it remains the case that views that are formally espoused and preached do not correspond with what is practiced in the name of authority and power by the formal hierarchical structures. There is a profound chasm between what the Church proclaims as the meaning and purpose of its existence on the one hand and the manifestation of that purpose in terms of organizational structure and practice on the other. Thus the Church "finds itself in the compromising position of acting antithetically to its own avowed nature"(Ketcham 1978:160).

This problem may be a difficult one to understand for those involved in Church circles, but in the world of organizational consulting it is an everyday bread-and-butter issue that is easily tackled by a little systematic reflection. Often, the hardest thing for a secular organization is to define "purpose" in a way that is acceptable to everyone who works there. Once that hurdle has been surmounted, it only remains to formulate the kind of strategy that is directed to achieving that purpose and to create or redesign an organizational structure within which that strategy can be effectively implemented (Fritz 1994). The Church has no problem with purpose, but the challenge posed by the realities of secular organizational change is a call to abandon the set certainties of institutional structures that are cast in the concrete of tradition, to realize that in order to remain true to its primary task of evangelizing cultures the Church has to be open to the need for institutional structural change so that its structures serve to foster the Kingdom rather than hinder its realization. The call to conversion is a call to repent, to turn away from the reliance on organizational authority and power, and to seek to witness as a community.

Organizations in the secular world increasingly seek a rationale for their existence. Milton Friedman's view that business is all about making money for shareholders makes little sense when business organizations clearly exist for the purpose of making something else; in any event, this view was tenable only when at least a majority of other stakeholders found their needs for security and meaning satisfied by the organization. But the advent of change and uncertainty during the last two decades has meant that sensitivity to purpose has become a requirement for organizations seeking to make an adequate response to external circumstances. The identification of purpose in terms that mean something to the people who have to realize it is the hallmark of organizations who seek to be "virtuous" (Collier 1995).[9]

The articulation of organizational purpose can be done only with reference to the values that underpin the organizational culture. It is at this level that the challenge to conversion comes. The values of the gospel are also those that are appropriate to the virtuous organization, because they are the values that will lead the organization to seek the welfare of all stakeholders—not merely shareholders, but also customers and supplier, employees, the wider community, and the future generations whose welfare depends on the preservation of the natural environment. But the challenge presented by the gospel becomes starker when it is a question of establishing priorities between competing stakeholder needs. Our priorities are clear. We are asked to make an "option for the poor," to attend specifically to the welfare of those without a voice and without the means to protect themselves from the actions of organizations who, occasionally but not often unwittingly, despoil the property, the health, and the social systems of the powerless. The challenge to conversion for organizations is not so much the abandonment of power, but the abandonment of its misuse and the commitment to the pursuit of the good. Only then can we truly say:

there are no more distinctions between

Jew and Greek.

slave and free.

but all of you are one in Christ Jesus (Gal. 3:28)[10]

# Conclusion

It is said that every problem has a history. This book has told the story of the relationship between "church" and the Western "world," a relationship that progressed from a complicity that made mission impossible to a fracture that made mission irrelevant in a culture that no longer needed religion. The gap was further widened by the reaction of a church that became increasingly suspicious of everything secular and increasingly intent on self-preservation. Complicity, in other words, was replaced by mutual mistrust.

But in the last fifty years there have been changes that culminated in the work of the Second Vatican Council, changes that articulated new visions, generated new understandings, and sowed the seeds of a new purpose. The Council was the work of the Spirit that constantly "renews the face of the earth," but such renewal needs a human response, and in this case it was not forthcoming. Although many Church organizations did undergo profound structural and cultural changes, the hierarchical Church had little idea of what was required to implement and carry forward the sense of purpose that was the legacy of the Council. It responded by a continuing mistrust that has manifested itself as restorationism.

If the Roman Catholic Church is to survive, it needs to recover and make explicit the missionary identity implicit

in the perspective of Vatican II. We believe that the understanding of mission as encounter holds the key to that
recovery. It is in the encounter with the secular world,
specifically with the "culture of economism," that the
Church can learn how to become the missionary Church
envisaged by Vatican II. In the first instance it can learn
how to transform its organizational structures to enable it
to fulfill that purpose. But at a deeper level, that encounter
will also enable the institutional Church to become aware
of its own need of "conversion." Unless the Church itself
embodies the values of the Kingdom in its organizational
life, it cannot preach that kingdom to others.

The missionary encounter between church and world
takes place at one level every day. Millions of Christians
work in secular organizations, many Christians fill positions
of responsibility. They move between the religious and secular contexts. They constitute an interface between the two
worlds in a way that makes encounter possible; in theory
they should allow each world to help the other to find what
is needed for integrity. Secular organizations need to recover meaning; they seek a value base that will allow them to
serve as well as to profit. The Roman Catholic Church
needs to develop a management structure characterized by
transformational leadership, participative structures, and
communication networks, and it needs to find ways of
implementing this change that are consistent with the values articulated in the concerns of the contextual theologies.
Both need to become "virtuous organizations."

The missionary encounter is not an encounter
between individuals; it is an encounter between two ways
of being and living. It has therefore to take place between
groups and communities. This places a great responsibility on the church to create the community structures
that embody the values of the Kingdom. Such groups,
whether informal or institutional, whether at a parish or
at an international level, can bring to the encounter the

concerns of the contextual theologies that articulate the message of the Kingdom, and the secular organizations can in turn bring their deepening understanding of the management of virtuous organizations. In the encounter, each is challenged to conversion: the church can become a better church, and secular organizations can become better organizations. In each case, the meaning of the word *better* is different, because in the encounter each sees in the other what is lacking for the realization of its own identity. This process of mutual conversion is the way to a nonviolent integration of our fragmented world, so that all things may be reconciled, whether on earth or in heaven (Col.1:20).

This book has used the heuristic of "value dilemmas" to characterize the problems of encounter between church and world. That encounter in itself represents a value dilemma, that between the religious and the secular. The encounter between these two values is exemplified in the writing of this book, and it has happened by bringing together the personal concerns and experiences of the two coauthors. One of the authors is committed primarily to the transformation of the organizational culture of the secular world in the socioeconomic sphere, the other to the transformation of the organizational culture of the Roman Catholic Church. What we have discovered in the process of writing this book is in fact very simple: each has to learn from the best the other has to offer. The Church as an organization has to look at itself in the context of all the research and best practice that goes on in the world of secular organizations, and secular organizations have to act taking into account the context of fundamental concerns that the Church retains as "espoused" theory in spite of the difficulties of translating theory into practice.

Our hope is that in the writing of this book we have created a synergy that will allow readers to find in this text guidelines by which they can navigate their own particular territory. This task is not a lonely one but a shared search that draws together people of good will in any walk of life and in any culture who reach out toward a world of justice, peace and love. It is this hope that Christian believers express when we pray together the prayer that Jesus taught us: "Thy Kingdom come."

# Notes

---

## Chapter 1: The Crisis of Western Culture and Christian Mission

1.   See, e.g., Bosch (1991), Heller and Feher (1988), Smart (1992). We do not propose to cast the analysis here in terms of the shift from modernism to postmodernism, partly because we believe that disputes as to the content of these concepts render them inexact and therefore less useful than they might be. See, e.g., Giddens (1990). But others use these concepts as heuristics: for instance, "Modernism refers to a culture whose unifying theme is the quest of the individual for self-fulfillment and empowerment. Postmodernism extends this notion to celebrate the sheer willfulness and instinctual impulse of individual action" (Alexander and Seidman 1990:232).

2.   We use the word *institution* throughout this book in the sense of "a social organization which, through the operation of tradition, custom or legal constraint, tends to create durable and routinized patterns of behavior" (Hodgson 1988:10). This definition would include the family, for instance, as well as the more formal types of organization.

3.   Bernard Lonergan (1971) sees the classicist conception of a universal and permanent culture as justifying the view that there can be only one universally valid theology.

4.　This is the perspective of "critical theory" as expounded in the work of the Frankfurt School. See, for instance, Habermas (1976).

5.　These two words will be used here in their etymological meaning of "uniting" and "separating," respectively.

6.　Mary Bateson (1984) reports discussions between her father, Gregory Bateson, and her mother, Margaret Mead, on how to tackle this issue.

7.　"Ethos" is defined by Mary Bateson (1984:81) as "the pervasiveness and congruity of style within a system that make any culture more than a list of traits and institutions."

8.　For E. F. Schumacher: "Economics plays a central role in shaping the activities of the modern world, inasmuch as it supplies the criteria of what is 'economic' and what is 'uneconomic,' and there is no other set of criteria that exercises a greater influence over the actions of individuals and groups" (1974:33).

9.　See e.g., John Paul II's encyclical *Laborem Exercens*.

10. These subjective levels of thought (see e.g. Lonegan 197) parallel the account given by critical realism of a differentiated and stratified objective world. Bhaskar (1979) identifies three levels of reality. There is the world of the empirical that we experience, there is the world of events that we may or may not experience, and there is the underlying world of causal or generative mechanisms, tendencies, forces, laws, or powers.

11. In historical terms, this represents a shift from the medieval view of society as hierarchically differentiated, with all spheres of activity teleologically arranged, to a view of society as functionally differentiated. The interpretation of the economy then shifted from an action-nexus to an autonomous functional nexus, a self-organizing system, no longer under the demands of ethics (Wieland 1994).

12. The hegemony of neoclassical economics has a great deal to do with the self-selectivity of Anglo-American—that is, English-speaking—thinking about economics. Theorists with alternative views, such as for instance Fredrich List, have been ignored because in the Anglo-American worldview: "Political economics becomes an essentially religious question, subject

to the standard drawback of any religion—the failure to understand why people outside the faith might act as they do" (Fallows 1993:62).

13. His "hidden agenda" was to legitimize the free and unfettered workings of the market of his day by showing that the workings of the market are rooted in human motivations that are beneficial because they are universal.

14. Late twentieth-century natural science accepts neither the closed world of Newtonian physics nor the fact-value distinction of positivism. The core paradigm of economics has not yet caught up with physics in this respect.

15. Ideology should be thought of not as any deliberate distortion of the truth designed to create Marx's "false consciousness." It is rather a partial, selective, or slanted representation of reality genuinely believed in by those who create and disseminate it.

16. Public goods, for instance, such as national defense, must be provided by a central authority.

17. This understanding encourages us to see individuals as real, as the ultimate conceptual building blocks of the economy. Social aggregates—communities, societies, cultures—are then merely mental constructs.

18. For instance, the Irish language has no single verb that denotes possession; the consequences of this influenced traditional cultural practices on ownership, hospitality, and property.

19. This is a view clearly grounded in traditions of critical realism (e.g., Bhaskar 1979) rather than in those of social constructionism (e.g., Berger and Luckman 1966).

20. For instance, what if our basic understanding of argument is that "argument is war" (Lakoff and Johnson 1980)? We then act out an argument as conflict. Suppose, however, that our metaphor for argument is that "argument is dance." Our metaphorical understanding of the nature of argument would then be very different, and so would our experience of an argument situation.

21. Not all cultures base their metaphorical systems on an up/down axis. Alternatives are concepts of balance, of centrality, of an active-passive alternation (Lakoff and Johnson 1980).

22. Economics works with two conceptions of equilibrium: one is Alfred Marshall's notion of the mechanistic balance between the forces of demand and supply within the market; the other is the image of harmony and order that results from the choices of rational agents, which is inherent in the thinking of Leon Walras and Vilfredo Pareto.

23. This is often done in ordinary-language speech by the rhetorical device of metonymy-the use of one entity to refer to another (Lakoff and Johnson 1980). Nixon bombed Hanoi, not people: companies, not people, raise prices; Wall Street, not people, panics. Metonymy allows us to depersonalize and hence to dehumanize.

24. This is the figure for the United States and the United Kingdom. The figure for Japan is much lower.

### Chapter 2: Culture's Consequences

1. Toynbee continues: "Twenty-three centuries before the appearance of these eighteenth and nineteenth-century philosophers, an Hellenic man of science, Empedocles, attributed the changes in the face of the Universe, of which we are empirically aware, to the alternate ebb and flow of two forces which are complementary to one another and at the same time antithetical; an integrating force which he calls love and a disintegrating force which he calls hate."

2. This view owes most to Gregory Bateson (1958, 1972), but it also owes something to Max Boisot's (1995) recent work on the production and exchange of knowledge in a social system—notably his idea of the Social Learning Cycle. The "systems" view of culture is not the only one, but it is the one that has the greatest heuristic potential in this context.

3. The application of cybernetics to culture was originally Bateson's idea, but it has been extended and applied to the study of both national and organizational cultures by Charles Hampden-Turner (1990, 1994).

4. This idea is explained more fully in Hampden-Turner (1994:19).

5. The meaning of the word *synergy* is taken from the Greek "synergos"—to work with. The notion of managing dilemmas is based on the work of Charles Hampden-Turner (1990, 1994).

6. Modern technology has the effect of interposing an artificial environment between a given social group and its immediate habitat, so that people from what were originally very diverse cultures find themselves in increasingly similar physical circumstances (Boisot 1995:315).

7. The successors of these companies are the "agribusinesses" that control production and prices in world food markets.

8. Attempts to impose accountability procedures on transnational corporations have largely met with failure. The UN Center for Transnational Corporations was closed down after the Earth Summit because of pressure from large Western industrial nations.

9. One of the reasons why unemployment is less in the United States is that labor has taken a substantial cut in real wages since the beginning of the 80s.

10. Charles Handy (1989) envisages the organization of the future as a "shamrock" having three categories of workers: the core workers, the contractual fringe, and the flexible "reserve army" of part-time, low-pay, low-status workers.

11. This paragraph relies heavily on Hawken (1993).

Chapter 3: The Church and Economism

1. Perhaps it is unwise to generalize about a reality as complex as Christianity, with all the pluralism of its various churches and communities. We speak here about the community to which we belong as Roman Catholics: those who belong to sister churches and Christian communities must consider whether what we see, feel, experience, and hope applies also to them.

2. Because of the Constantinian Settlement, the Roman Empire finally accepted Christianity as legitimate.

3. The early church was aware of the ambiguity of power. The "give to Caesar what is Caesar's and to God what is God's" recognized secular power as God-given and therefore good. But on the other hand, Nero, as the embodiment of a diabolic state, is seen in the Book of Revelation as the "Beast" opposed to God. This should have been enough warning for the Christian community to keep its distance from institutions that exercise and accumulate power. There is here the basis of a theological reflection on the structural ambiguity of any human institution—ecclesial institutions included.

4. This process is still happening; the Protestant churches of England and Ireland are still "established."

5. The ecclesial paradigm within Roman Catholicism has been undergoing a profound change. The Second Vatican Council (1962–65) triggered in the Church a deep process of rethinking and reassessing its own identity. It is therefore necessary when speaking about the Roman Catholic Church to distinguish between the pre–Vatican II and the post–Vatican II period. For the time being, we will focus on the pre–Vatican II paradigm, which is challenged today but which is far from dead. In fact, it is still in many ways the dominant paradigm of the central administration of the Church.

6. This apparently has deep biblical roots: the languages divide in Babel after the attempt to scale heaven, whereas the language barrier is overcome with the outpouring of the Spirit at Pentecost.

7. This same process, the inability to deal with the diversity of cultural contexts and languages, is also what lay behind the great divisions of Christianity: the Monophysite schism, the division of East and West, and the Reformation.

8. Canon Law still attributes those powers exclusively to priests.

9. The Pope has recently made it clear not only that the possibility of the ordination of women should be discarded but that there should be no further discussion of the issue. This pronouncement is declared to be infallible. The policy is also maintained of teaching candidates for the priesthood in single-sex institutions.

10. Quoted in Fairbanks 1995:133.

## Chapter 4: The Second Vatican Council:
## From Power Games to Powerlessness

1. In this context the term is used in two of Kuhn's three senses (Masterman 1970). The paradigm shift that happened as a result of Vatican II was both sociological and metaphysical in the sense of "a new way of seeing" (Kuhn 1962:117–21).

2. The media shorthand for these structures is "the Vatican." This is in a way an unhappy generalization, because there are many, even within the Curia, who support the ecclesial openness of the Second Vatican Council. However, within the Vatican, power currently belongs to a core group intent on controlling the life of the Church and resisting change, and they are supported by many within the hierarchy around the world. In a real way the Vatican itself is polarized, but the lack of transparency makes it difficult to map adherences.

3. French theologians such as Henri de Lubac, Yves Congar, and Jean Danielou were in the forefront of this development.

4. The call to the abandonment of power was signified by the "prophetic gestures" of the abandonment of traditional trappings of papal and episcopal power—the "sedia gestatoria" and "noble guard," the "tiara"—as well as by the replacing of episcopal rings by a simple gold band.

5. Bevans (1992) gives a comprehensive account of the criteria by which contextual theology can be judged as "orthodox."

6. There are other forms of contextual theology that answer to other concerns; for instance, "creationist" theology answers the ecological concern for the survival of the earth.

7. Margaret Thatcher's statement that "there is no such thing as society" characterizes the stance of a culture that has ceased to recognize the value of community.

8. All this brings to the fore the ambiguity of the notion of empowerment that is so often used by contextual theologies. The paradigm shift that we are experiencing should not be seen simply as a power shift. We believe that an essential element of the new organizational culture needed in the Roman Catholic Church is the total abandonment of power games. The Church has to transform the world not from a position of

power, but by believing in the transforming challenge of powerlessness, which is none other than the challenge of the cross.

9. The best known and the best organized of these conservative groups is Opus Dei. The influence of this organization has grown rapidly during the present pontificate. It is said
that it now controls the Congregation of Bishops (which is
responsible for appointing all bishops), the Congregation of
the Canonization of Saints, as well as the Press Center of the
Vatican. See Arbuckle (1993:52) for an account of the role of
this and other movements.

## Chapter 5: Christian Mission to the Culture of Economism

1. *Ad Gentes Divinitus*—Vatican II's document on mission—remained a nonintegrated document with a bit of the
new and a bit of the old: also, it did not take into account the
theology of non-Christian religious, which was in full development during the time of the Council itself. In particular, it did
not recognize the secularized West as mission territory, for the
Church had already been implanted there.

2. This is the post-Kantian "turn to the subject" that
allowed theologians such as Lonergan to argue that "objectiv-
ity is simply the consequence of authentic subjectivity"
(1971:265). It also allowed the development of a "new ontol-
ogy" grounded in the work of Husserl and Heidegger. Karl
Rahner, Rudolf Bultmann, Martin Buber, and John Macquarrie
belong in this tradition within theology (Ketcham 1978:ix).

3. Perhaps the best example is the document on the Church
in the World (*Gaudium et Spes*). According to Shorter (1994:69)
the document on mission, *Ad Gentes*, "contained the seeds of a
new mission paradigm... later to be called inculturation."

4. This is an ongoing process that has taken shape in the
variety of contextual theologies that need to be brought to
some kind of underlying unity. We believe that the understanding of mission as encounter can provide that unifying
principle.

5. Although the contextual theologies are groping with
this kind of model (for example, the theology of inculturation),

it is the reflection on mission as dialogue and encounter that is more surely grounded in experience.

6. "Fara,"a corruption of the word *Father*, had long since lost its English roots. It was a generic name given to all missionaries, men and women alike, as an ethnic group. "Fara" were thus distinguished from "Similinga," the "white" ethnic group.

7. Ambiguity does not mean simplistically that organizations are evil. It means that they are a complex interaction of symbolic (integrating, healing, life-giving) and diabolic (destructive, disintegrating, diseasing, deadly) structures and structural tendencies. From a theological point of view, we connect the symbolic in structures to the liberating action of God's Spirit or to the reconciling presence of the Kingdom of God; we attribute the diabolic structural tendencies to sin or the shadow side of humanity that has not yet fallen under the liberating dynamic of the Kingdom of God.

8. The fast-changing demands of an increasingly complex global environment have generated new organizational perodyms and new models of management. Organizations are becoming more open, less hierachical and more relational. See e.g., Ghoshal and Bartlett 1998.

9. Alisdair MacIntyre (1984) develops the notion of virtue as "practice" in a way that can be applied to organizations. See also Fukuyama (1995) on the concept of an "ethical habit."

10. It is amazing to notice that Paul in this text points precisely to the fractures that we have found as being the main negative consequences of violent integration. What Paul points to is to integration through fidelity to the reconciling Spirit who gives freedom to the believer.

# References Cited

Alexander, Jeffrey C., and Steven Seidman, eds. 1990. *Culture and Society: Contemporary Debates.* Cambridge: Cambridge University Press.

Arbuckle, Gerald A. 1990. *Earthing the Gospel.* Maryknoll: Orbis Books.

———. 1993. *Refounding the Church: Dissent for Leadership.* London: Geoffrey Chapman.

Argyris, Chris, and Donald Schon. 1978. *Organizational Learning.* Reading, Mass: Addison-Wesley.

Bateson, Gregory. 1958. *Naven.* 2d ed. Stanford: Stanford University Press.

———. 1972. *Steps to An Ecology of Mind.* London: Chandler Publishing Co.

Bateson, Mary Catherine. 1984. *With a Daughter's Eye.* New York: Washington Square Press.

Bausch, William. 1988. Ministry: *Traditions, Tensions and Transitions.* Mystic: Twenty-Third Publications.

Benedict, Ruth. 1935. *Patterns of Culture.* London: Routledge & Kegan Paul.

Benton, R.Jr. 1990. *A Hermeneutic Approach to Economics.* In Economics as Discoursem ed. Samuels.

Berger, Peter, and Thomas Luckman. 1966. *The Social Construction of Reality.* Garden City: Doubleday & Co.

Bevans, Stephen B. 1992. *Models of Contextual Theology.* Maryknoll: Orbis Books.

Bhaskar, Roy. 1979. *The Possibility of Naturalism.* Sussex Brighton: Harvester Press.

Bilmoria, Diana, David L. Cooperrider, et al. 1994. A Call to Organizational Scholarship. The Organization Dimensions of Global Change: No Limits to Cooperation. *Journal of Management Inquiry* 4:1: 71–95.

Black, Max. 1962. *Models and Metaphors.* Ithaca: Cornell University.

Boff, Leonardo. 1985. *Church, Charism and Power: Liberation Theology and the Institutional Church.* New York: Crossroads.

Boisot, Max. 1995. *Information Space.* London: Routledge.

Bosch, David J. 1991. *Transforming Mission: Paradigm Shifts in Theology of Mission.* Maryknoll: Orbis Books.

Bourdieu, Pierre. 1990. *In Other Words: Essays Towards a Reflexive Sociology.* Cambridge: Polity Press.

Buber, Martin. 1937. *I and Thou.* Trans. by R. G. Smith. Edinburgh: T. & T. Clark.

Capra, Fritz. 1983. *The Turning Point.* London: HarperCollins.

Chung, Hyun Kyung. 1990. *Struggle to Be the Sun Again: Introducing Asian Womens' Theology.* Maryknoll: Orbis Books.

Collier, Jane. 1990. *The Culture of Economism: An Exploration of Barriers to Faith as Praxis.* Frankfurt: Peter Lang.

———. 1992. *Economics and Contemporary Culture. In The Gospel and Our Culture,* ed. Montefiore.

———. 1995. The Virtuous Organization. *Business Ethics: A European Review* 4:4: 143-49.

Collins, Mary. 1987. *Worship: Renewal to Practice.* Washington, D.C.: The Pastoral Press.

Cooper, Norman P. 1993. *Collaborative Ministry: Communion, Contention, Commitment.* Mahwah: Paulist Press.

Coser, Lewis A. and Bernard Rosenberg, eds. 1969. *Sociological Theory.* London: Macmillan.

de Romana, Alfredo L. 1989. The Autonomous Economy. Part 2: Impoverishing Economic Growth. *Interculture* 22:4. Issue 105.

Eichner, Alfred S. 1993. *Why Economics Is Not Yet a Science.* London: Macmillan.

Eliot, T. S. 1948. *Notes Towards the Definition of Culture.* London: Faber & Faber.

Elliott, Charles. 1987. *Comfortable Compassion.* London: Hodder & Stoughton.

Esteban, Rafael. 1994. Evangelization, Culture and Spirituality. *The Way,* 34:4: 273-82.

Esteban, Rafael. 1995. An Experience of Priesthood in Two Continents. *The Way Supplement* 83: 25-33.

Fabella, Virginia, and Mercy Amba Oduyoye. 1988. *With Passion and Compassion: Third World Women Doing Theology.* Maryknoll: Orbis Books.

Fairbanks, Sarah Ann. 1995. Liturgical Preaching by Women: A New Sign of Salvation. *The Way Supplement* 83: 131–40.

Fallows, James. 1993. How the World Works. *The Atlantic Monthly.* December, pp. 61–87.

Folbre, Nancy, and Heidi Hartmann. 1988. The Rhetoric of Self-Interest: Ideology and Gender in Economic Theory. In *The Consequences of Economic Rhetoric,* ed. Klamer et al.

Freire, Paulo. 1970. *A Pedagogy of the Oppressed.* Harmondsworth: Penguin.

Fritz, Robert. 1994. *Corporate Tides.* London: Butterworth-Heinemann.

Fukuyama, Francis. 1995. *Trust.* Harmondsworth: Penguin.

Geertz, C. 1973. *The Interpretation of Cultures.* New York: Basic Books.

Ghoshal, Sumantra, and Christopher Bartlett. 1994. Changing the Role of Top Management: Beyond Strategy to Purpose. *Harvard Business Review.* November-December, pp. 79–89.

——. 1995a. Changing the Role of Top Management: Beyond Structure to Processes. *Harvard Business Review,* January-February, pp. 87–96.

——. 1995b. Changing the Role of Top Management: Beyond Systems to People". *Harvard Business Review*. May-June, pp. 132–42.

——. 1998. The Individualized Corporation: A Fundamentally New Approach to Management. London: Heinemann.

Giddens, Anthony. 1990. *The Consequences of Modernity.* Cambridge: Polity Press.

Gutierrez, Gustavo. 1973. *A Theology of Liberation.* New York: Orbis Books.

Habermas, Jürgen. 1976. *Legitimation Crisis.* London: Heinemann.

Hampden-Turner, Charles. 1990. *Corporate Culture.* London: Hutchinson.

——. 1994. Charting the Corporate Mind. London: Blackwell.

Handy, Charles. 1989. *The Age of Unreason.* London: Hutchinson, Business Books.

Hawken, Paul. 1993. *The Ecology of Commerce: How Business Can Save the Planet.* London: Weidenfeld & Nicholson.

Heilbronner, Robert. 1988. Rhetoric and Ideology. In *The Consequences of Economic Rhetoric*, ed. Klamer, et al.

——. 1990. Economics as Ideology. In *Economics Discourse*, ed. Samuels.

Heller A., and F. Feher. 1988. *The Postmodern Political Condition.* Cambridge: Polity Press.

Henderson, Willie. 1982. Metaphor in Economics. *Economics* 18:4: 147–53.

Henderson, Willie, Tony Dudley-Evans, and Roger Backhouse, eds. 1993. *Economics and Language*. London: Routledge.

Hesse, Mary. 1980. *Revolutions and Reconstructions in the Philosophy of Science.* Sussex Brighton: Harvester Press.

Hodgson, Geoffrey M. 1988. *Economics and Institutions.* Cambridge: Polity Press.

Hofstede, Geert. 1980. *Culture's Consequences: International Differences in Work-Related Values.* Beverly Hills: Sage Publications.

——. 1991. *Cultures and Organizations: Software of the Mind.* Maidenhead, Eng.: McGraw-Hill.

Hutchinson, Terence W. 1977. *Knowledge and Ignorance in Economics.* Oxford: Blackwell.

John Paul II. 1984. *Laborem Exercens.* An Encyclical on Human Work. London: Catholic Truth Society.

———. 1988. *Mulieris Dignitatem.* An Apostolic Letter on the Dignity and Vocation of women. London: Catholic Truth Society.

Kaplan, Robert D. 1994. The Coming Anarchy. *The Atlantic Monthly.* February, pp. 44-76.

Ketcham, Charles B. 1978. *A Theology of Encounter.* University Park and London: The Pennsylvania Press.

King, Ursula. 1994. *Feminist Theology from the Third World: A Reader.* London: SPCK.

Klamer, Arjo, Donald N. McCloskey, and Robert M. Solow, Robert M. eds. 1988. *The Consequences of Economic Rhetoric.* Cambridge: Cambridge University Press.

Kluckhorn, Clyde. 1969. The Study of Culture. In *Sociological Theory,* ed. Coser and Rosenberg.

Kuhn, Thomas. 1962. *The Structure of Scientific Revolutions.* Chicago: University of Chicago Press.

Lakatos, Imre, and Alan Musgrave eds. 1970. *Criticism and the Growth of Knowledge.* Cambridge: Cambridge University Press.

Lakoff, George, and Mark Johnson. 1980. *Metaphors We Live By.* Chicago: University of Chicago Press.

Lavoie, Don, ed. 1990. *Economics and Hermeneutics.* London: Routledge.

Lens, Sidney. 1970. *The Military-Industrial Complex.* London: Stanmore Press.

Lewis, Alan, and Karl-Erik Warneryd, eds. 1994. *Ethics and Economic Affairs.* London: Routledge.

Lonergan, Bernard. 1971. *Method in Theology.* London: Darton, Longman, and Todd.

Mabey, Christopher and Paul Iles eds. 1994. *Managing Learning.* London: Routledge.

McCloskey, Donald N. 1990. Storytelling in Economics. In *Economics and Hermenentics,* ed. Lavoie.

———. 1992. *If You're So Smart: The Narrative of Economic Expertise*. Chicago: University of Chicago Press.

———. 1994. *Knowledge and Persuasion in Economics*. Cambridge: Cambridge University Press.

MacIntyre, Alisdair. 1984. *After Virtue*. 2d ed. Notre Dame: University of Notre Dame Press.

Maki, Uskali. 1993. Two Philosophies of the Rhetoric of Economics. In *Economics and Language*, ed. Henderson et al.

Marcel, Gabriel. 1951. *The Mystery of Being*. Vol.2. London: The Harvill Press.

Marshall, Alfred. 1898. Mechanical and Biological Analogies in Economics. Reprinted in Pigou, A. C. 1925. *Memorials of Alfred Marshall*. London: Macmillan.

Masterman, Margaret. 1970. The Nature of a Paradigm. In *Criticism and the Growth of Knowledge*, ed. Lakatos and Musgrave.

Montefiore, Hugh. 1992. *The Gospel and Our Culture*. London: Cassels.

Nelson, Julie. 1992. Gender, Metaphor, and the Definition of Economics. *Economics and Philosophy* 8:1: 103–25.

Panikkar, Raimon. 1981. *The Unknown Christ of Hinduism: Towards An Ecumenical Christophany*. Maryknoll: Orbis Books.

Polanyi, Michael. 1958. *Personal Knowledge*. Chicago: University of Chicago Press.

Provost James H. ed. 1984. *The Church as Communion*. Washington D.C.: Canon Law Society of America.

Rich, Adrienne. 1977. *Of Women Born*. London: Virago.

Richards, I. A. 1936. *The Philosophy of Rhetoric*. Oxford: Oxford University Press.

Samuels, Warren J. ed. 1990. *Economics as Discourse*. Boston: Kluwer Academic Press.

———. 1992. *Essays on the Methodology and Discourse of Economics*. London: Macmillan.

Schumacher, E. F. 1974. *Small Is Beautiful*. London: Abacus.

Schüssler Fiorenza, Elisabeth. 1993. *Discipleship of Equals*. London: SCM Press.

Segundo, J. L. 1974. *A Theology for Artisans of a New Humanity.* New York: Orbis Books.

Sen, Amartya. 1982 *Choice Welfare and Measurement.* Oxford: Blackwell.

———. 1984. *Resources, Values and Development.* Oxford: Blackwell.

Senge, Peter. 1994. The Leader's New Work. In *Managing Learning,* ed. Mabey and Iles.

Shiva, Vandana. 1989. *Staying Alive: Women, Ecology and Development.* London: Zed Books.

Shorter, Aylward. 1988. *Towards a Theology of Inculturation.* Maryknoll: Orbis Books.

———. 1994. *Evangelization and Culture.* London: Geoffrey Chapman.

Smart, B. 1992. *Modern Conditions, Postmodern Controversies.* London: Routledge.

Sofield, Loughlan, and Carroll Juliano. 1987. *Collaborative Ministry.* Notre Dame: Ave Maria.

Steingard, David S., and Dale E. Fitzgibbon. 1995. Challenging the Juggernaut of Globalization: A Manifesto of Academic Praxis. *Journal of Organizational Change Management* 8:4: 30–54.

Thistlethwaite, Susan Brooks. 1989. *Sex, Race and God: Christian Feminism in Black and White.* New York: Crossroad.

Toynbee, Arnold. 1988. *A Study of History.* Abr. ed. London: Oxford University Press and Thames and Hudson.

Whorf, Benjamin Lee. 1956. *Language, Thought and Reality.* Cambridge: MIT Press.

Wieland, Josef. 1994. Economy and Ethics in Functionally Differentiated Societies. In *Ethics and Economic Affairs,* ed. Lewis and Warneryd.